‘GATHERING OF THE CLANS’

THE CLAN LINE STEAMERS LTD.

CLAN MACTAVISH of 1949. *(J.K. de Vries Jnr.).*

'GATHERING OF THE CLANS'

THE HISTORY OF THE CLAN LINE STEAMERS LTD

by

N.L. MIDDLEMISS

SHIELD PUBLICATIONS LTD
NEWCASTLE UPON TYNE
GREAT BRITAIN

ISBN 1 871128 00 5

Published by Shield Publications Ltd., Newcastle upon Tyne

Printed by Athenæum Press Ltd., Newcastle upon Tyne

P R E F A C E

Mr Middlemiss has painstakingly completed an account of the Clan Line fleet since its beginnings in the last century, through the two great wars, to its eventual run-down at the start of this decade. Whilst the passing of all these fine ships is sad, their evolution over the years is a great tribute to those who designed and built them, as well as to those who served in them as seafarers. It is heartening to reflect that this accumulated knowledge and experience has not disappeared, but has contributed to the next generation of ocean transport - the container era. Clan Line's trades and skills, along with those of other well known British Shipping Companies, transferred to Overseas Containers Limited, now P&OCL, which continues to operate successfully today as the largest British cargo liner company.

Cayzer

P R E F A C E

[illegible] of the [illegible]

[illegible]

through the [illegible]

staff [illegible] Walton [illegible] of all [illegible]

ships [illegible], the [illegible] over the [illegible] a [illegible]

tribute to [illegible] designed [illegible] as [illegible]

[illegible] who [illegible] in them [illegible]

[illegible] that [illegible]

not disappeared, but has [illegible] the [illegible]

[illegible]

and [illegible] with [illegible]

[illegible]

[illegible] which continues to operate [illegible]

the largest [illegible]

[illegible]

[illegible]

CONTENTS

AUTHOR

Norman Lea Middlemiss was born at South Shields in 1945 and was educated at Tynemouth High School and Newcastle University, graduating with an Honours degree in Mathematics in 1966. Since then he has worked as a Systems Analyst and Computer Consultant writing software for a wide variety of applications. Systems of a maritime nature that he has seen to completion include the Seawolf missile system as carried by the Type 22 and Type 23 frigates, and the first shipyard computerised production planning system in the world for the Southwick, Sunderland shipyard of Austin & Pickersgill Ltd., home of the very successful SD14 'Liberty' replacement vessel. He also lectures on Computing at Colleges and was formerly the Senior Lecturer in Computing for Ferranti Ltd. at Bracknell, training Royal and foreign naval officers and crews in computer systems.

The author has had several articles published in the magazines 'Ships Monthly' and 'Sea Chest', the magazine of his local World Ship Society Tyneside Branch of which he was a founder member in 1960.

ACKNOWLEDGEMENTS

'A Victorian Shipowner' by Augustus Muir and Mair Davies – a portrait of Sir Charles Cayzer, Baronet of Gartmore, published by Cayzer, Irvine & Co. Ltd. in 1978.

'The Elusive Seagull' by E.P. Hoyt, published 1976 by Tandem Books.

'Last Cruise of the EMDEN' by E.P. Hoyt, published by White Lion Publishers Ltd. in 1975.

'In Dangers Hour' by G. Holman, published 1948 by Hodder & Stoughton Ltd.

'Early Victorian England' edited by G.M. Young, published 1963 by Oxford University Press.

'The Merchantmen' by R. Armstrong, published 1969 by Ernest Benn Ltd., London.

'Sea Breezes' May/June 1963.

'Clan Line in the Great War' by Sir Archibald Spicer Hurd.

'Clansman' and 'British and Commonwealth Reviews' – House Magazines.

Clan Line and British & Commonwealth Annual Reports and Accounts.

I would like to thank also Ronald French, Harold Appleyard, George Scott, Bernard Lawley and Douglas Kinghorn, E. Ridley, N.G. Tracey, J.G. Hall, P. Butcher, G. Waring and Tyne & Wear Museums Services for their help in preparing this research, and Diane Redman for the word-processing.

LIST OF ILLUSTRATIONS

24. CLAN MURRAY of 1918 photographed in Table Bay was broken up at Bo'ness in 1952. *(W.S.P.L.).*
25. CLAN MACNAIR was completed by Ayrshire Dockyard and broken up at Blyth in 1952. *(B. Feilden).*
26. CLAN MACDOUGALL of 1929 and CLAN MACDONALD were the first company vessels with diesel engines. *(B. Feilden).*
27. CLAN MACPHERSON of 1929 reverted to triple expansion steam engines. *(J. Clarkson).*
28. CLAN GRANT was completed in 1912 by Hawthorn, Leslie as PORT MACQUARIE and purchased in 1929. *(A. Duncan).*
29. CLAN COLQUHOUN built in 1918 was formerly the White Star Line GALLIC before being purchased in 1933. *(B. Feilden).*
30. CLAN URQUHART was completed in 1911 as ARGYLLSHIRE for Scottish Shire Line and transferred to Clan Line in 1933. *(J. Clarkson).*
31. CLAN MACAULAY and CLAN MACARTHUR of 1936 were the start of a big building programme. *(F.R. Sherlock).*
32. CLAN CHATTAN of 1937 was a Malta convoy heroine. *(A. Duncan).*
33. CLAN CAMPBELL of 1937 was another Malta convoy heroine. *(A. Duncan).*
34. CLAN CAMERON of 1937 survived the war and was broken up at Hong Kong in 1959. *(F.R. Sherlock).*
35. CLAN MACRAE of 1942 was one of the CLAN CAMERON class but was completed as EMPIRE MIGHT. *(L. Baker).*
36. CLAN DAVIDSON of 1943 had a magnificent war record as a midget submarine depot ship. *(W.T. Hubbard).*
37. CLAN ALPINE built in 1942 as EMPIRE BARRIE at Sunderland and purchased in 1945 ended up in a paddy field near Chittagong in 1960 and was scrapped 'as lies'. *(B. Feilden).*
38. CLAN MACFADYEN was a 'Liberty' vessel completed in 1944 as SAMDERWENT and purchased in 1947. *(J. Clarkson).*
39. CLAN MACQUEEN was completed in 1942 as OCEAN VESPER and is photographed at Mombasa. *(Clansman).*
40. CLAN CHISHOLM built 1944 photographed entering Dublin. *(P. Sweeney).*
41. CLAN CAMPBELL built 1943 photographed in the English Channel. *(Skyfotos Ltd.).*
42. CLAN MACLENNAN completed in 1947 was one of 6 sisters. *(B. Feilden).*
43. CLAN MACLEAN of 1947 photographed at Vizaghapatnam. *(Clansman).*
44. CLAN SHAW of 1950, first of the 'S' class photographed in the Mersey. *(Mersey Photos).*
45. CLAN SINCLAIR of 1950 loading sugar from barges at Mauritius. *(Clansman).*
46. CLAN SUTHERLAND of 1951 seen on trials. *(W. Ralston Ltd.).*
47. CLAN SUTHERLAND lifting a 162-ton stator at Gladstone Dock, Liverpool. *(Stewart Bale Ltd.).*
48. CLAN STEWART of 1954 seen leaving the Tyne. *(G.R. Scott).*
49. CLAN ROBERTSON of 1954 at speed. *(Builders photograph).*

50. CLAN ROBERTSON of 1954 in the Mersey. *(B. Fielden).*
51. CLAN ROSS of 1956 seen on trials. *(Clansman).*
52. ARGYLLSHIRE of 1956 seen on trials. *(Clansman).*
53. The ill-fated AYRSHIRE of 1957. *(W. Ralston Ltd.).*
54. CLAN MATHESON of 1957 seen on trials. *(Clansman).*
55. CLAN MENZIES of 1958 seen leaving the Tyne in 1979 following pre-sale dry-docking inspection. *(G.R. Scott).*
56. CLAN MACINDOE of 1959 photographed in the English Channel. *(Skyfotos Ltd.).*
57. CLAN MACIVER of 1958 at Cape Town. *(Clansman).*
58. CLAN MACNAIR of 1962 at Cape Town. *(J.K. de Vries Jnr.).*
59. CLAN FRASER seen afloat in the Tyne after launching on 27th July 1961. *(Clansman).*
60. CLAN FINLAY seen afloat in the Tyne after launching on 29th June 1962. *(Clansman).*
61. CLAN FORBES fitting-out on the Tyne in May 1961. *(G.R. Scott).*
62. CLAN MACGILLIVRAY seen shortly before launch at Greenock Dockyard in May 1962 with a good general view of the yard. *(Clansman).*
63. CLAN RANALD being launched at Greenock Dockyard on 21st December 1964. *(Clansman).*
64. CLAN ALPINE, the last CLAN, being launched at Greenock Dockyard on 1st December 1966. *(Clansman).*
65. CLAN ALPINE photographed in the English Channel. *(Skyfotos Ltd.).*
66. CLAN ROSS of 1966 photographed in the English Channel. *(Skyfotos Ltd.).*
67. ARGYLLSHIRE passing Calshot Radar Station in Southampton Water in 1973. *(A. Greenway).*
68. Vittoria Dock, Birkenhead, as it is today with the last visible evidence of the CLAN LINE near the roof of the warehouse. *(Author).*

"CLAN LINE."

Steam to BOMBAY direct.

Steamers.	Steamers.
CLAN ALPINE.	CLAN LAMONT.
CLAN FRASER.	CLAN RANALD.
CLAN GORDON.	CLAN STUART.

The "CLAN LINE" Steamers are built expressly for the Indian Trade. The Saloons and State Cabins are on deck, and fitted with every requisite for comfort in tropical as well as in cold climates. Each Steamer carries a Surgeon and Stewardess.

FIRST-CLASS PASSAGE, THIRTY-FIVE GUINEAS.

Taking Goods at Through Rates for Coast Ports, Kurrachee and Persian Gulf, and issuing Through Bills of Lading.

The Splendid New Clyde-built Steam-Ship

CLAN STUART, 100 A I.

2200 Tons Gross Reg.; **280 H. P. Nominal;**

Will be despatched from

LIVERPOOL to BOMBAY on 26th APRIL, 1879.

For Freight and Passage apply to CAYZER, IRVINE & Co., Managing Owners, Liverpool; to the Agents, GELLATLY, HANKEY, SEWELL & Co., Manchester and Liverpool; to TURNBULL, MARTIN & Co., Glasgow; or

J. & R. GRANT,

1, LEADENHALL STREET, LONDON.

BILLS OF LADING.—"Eastern Trade" Form No 1, used for this Steamer, to be obtained at Messrs. HOWARD & JONES, Cullum Street; and Shipping Notes at Agents' Office.

Freight payable on delivery of Bills of Lading.

Goods must be distinctly marked for the Port of Destination.

"CLAN LINE" TO SOUTH AFRICA.

GLASGOW AND LIVERPOOL

TO

SOUTH AFRICAN PORTS.

THE magnificent Steamers of this Line will be despatched punctually

From GLASGOW on the 1st, and from LIVERPOOL on the 5th of every Month,

Or on the previous days when these dates fall on Sunday.

"CLAN GORDON,"

2091 TONS REGISTER, 1250 H.P. J. H. TORBOCK, COMMANDER.

WILL BE DESPATCHED PUNCTUALLY

From GLASGOW, on SATURDAY, 1st OCT., 1881.
From LIVERPOOL, on WEDNESDAY, 5th OCT., 1881.

THE "CLAN LINE" STEAMERS have been built and specially arranged for the Trade. The Saloons and State-Rooms are all on the Upper Deck, and are fitted with every requisite for comfort, in tropical as well as in cold climates.

The Rates of Passage Money include Steward's Fees, Bedding, Linen, and all Cabin Furniture, but does not include Wines or Spirits, which are not provided or sold on board any of the Clan Steamers. Passengers requiring such can ship what they require.

FIRST CLASS PASSAGE.

LIVERPOOL TO	*CAPE TOWN,*	*£25.*
Do.	*ALGOA BAY & MOSSEL BAY.*	*28.*
Do.	*NATAL, THE KOWIE, & EAST LONDON,*	*35.*
Do.	*MAURITIUS,*	*53.*

SPECIAL ARRANGEMENTS MADE FOR FAMILIES AND PARTIES.

One child under three years of age, free. When more than one under three years of age, each child additional will be charged one-quarter fare. Children over three years, and under ten years of age, half-fare; above ten years of age, full fare. Servants, two-thirds First-class Fare.

Each adult Passenger is allowed to take 5 cwt. of Baggage; Children paying half-fares, and Servants, 2 cwt.

Passengers embark at the Coy.'s Loading Berth, Morpeth Branch Dock, Birkenhead, to which place all Baggage should be sent, addressed to the Steamer, with Owner's name, to care of CAYZER, IRVINE, & CO. Baggage not wanted on the voyage, must be forwarded to Birkenhead, the day prior to the Steamer's sailing. The Company cannot be held responsible for Baggage under any circumstance whatever.

A deposit of £20 is required to secure a berth, the balance to be paid before embarking.

For Further Particulars, Plan of Cabins, &c., apply to

CAYZER, IRVINE, & CO.,

15 Great St. Helens, LONDON, E.C.; 98 Albert Square, MANCHESTER; 3 Old Churchyard, LIVERPOOL; and 109 Hope Street, GLASGOW.

"CLAN" LINE OF STEAMERS.

SAILING FORTNIGHTLY.

FROM **LIVERPOOL** FOR

COLOMBO, MADRAS & CALCUTTA,

BOMBAY & KURRACHEE,

CAPE TOWN, ALGOA BAY, EAST LONDON & NATAL.

These Steamers are specially arranged for the Passenger Trade: are lighted with the Electric Light, and fitted with every comfort for an Indian Voyage.

Surgeon and Stewardess carried.

For Rates of Passage Money, Plans of Cabins, and **further particulars** apply to

JAS SEARIGHT & CO.	CAPETOWN.
FINLAY, MUIR & CO.	BOMBAY.
AITKEN, SPENCE & CO.	COLOMBO.
GORDON, WOODROFFE & CO.	MADRAS.
FINLAY, MUIR & CO.	CALCUTTA.
CAYZER, IRVINE & CO.	GLASGOW.

"Clan" Line of Steamers.

PASSENGER LIST

OF THE STEAMER

"CLAN MACINTOSH"

FROM LIVERPOOL FOR

COLOMBO, MADRAS & CALCUTTA.

PASSENGERS embark at the MORPETH BRANCH DOCK, BIRKENHEAD, at 9 o'clock a.m., SUNDAY, 14th SEPTEMBER, 1890.

FOR FURTHER PARTICULARS APPLY TO

CAYZER, IRVINE & CO.,

GLASGOW, LONDON AND LIVERPOOL.

Passengers per "Clan Macintosh."

FOR PORT SAID.

Mr. T. R. Adamson
Mr. Shotton
Mrs. Shotton

FOR COLOMBO.

Mrs. McAlpine
and Child
Mr. Lushington
Mrs. Lushington
and Five Children
Miss Carey

FOR MADRAS.

Miss Valentine
Mr. J. Wallace
and Native Servant

Passengers per "Clan Macintosh."

FOR CALCUTTA.

Mr. R. E. Cooke
Mrs. Cooke
and Child
Mr. T. M. L. Thompson
Master Harry Thompson
Mr. J. G. Cummings
Mr. McNamara
Mr. Mesurier
Mr. C. Rippe
Mr. A. F. Rich
Mrs. Rich
Mr. Mansfield
Mrs. Davidson
and Child
Mr. Brand

W. McALLISTER, Commander.
Dr. BUCHANAN, Surgeon.
Mr. R. GEORGE, Chief Steward.
Mrs. FORREST, Stewardess.

1. INTRODUCTION.

It was in the mid fifties that I first became aware of the famous and much loved Clan Line funnel colours of twin red bands on a black background undergoing repairs at the then numerous Tyne ship repair yards. The post-war fleet became familiar to me as they continued to arrive for dry-docking and voyage repairs throughout the sixties and seventies, the last to be docked being CLAN MENZIES at Smiths Dock, North Shields for a brief pre-sale dry-docking inspection for her new owners in 1979. This included what I and many other people considered to be the most handsome vessels in the post-war fleet, CLAN ROBERTSON and CLAN ROSS. This was reinforced by the monthly arrivals of Clan Line vessels at Sunderland, which called there to unload sisal and other items for the local factories, on their way up the East Coast to Dundee to discharge jute. While Clan Line vessels were much more well known at Vittoria Dock, Birkenhead and King George V Dock, Glasgow, there was also a regular service up the East Coast from India calling at London, Hull, Middlesbrough, Sunderland and Dundee and/or Continental ports. The vessels were always well painted and maintained with a fine array of cargo-gear and were a credit to their owners and crew.

At the beginning of the sixties Swan, Hunter & Wigham Richardson Ltd. were building five of the class of sixteen 'Three-quarters aft' vessels. CLAN FERGUSSON was launched first on 3rd November, 1960 at the Wallsend yard and she was followed at four month intervals by CLAN FORBES, CLAN FRASER, CLAN FARQUHARSON and CLAN FINLAY. The five 'F' class were to provide a monthly service between Liverpool and the Persian Gulf, but the service was short-lived with CLAN FERGUSSON and CLAN FRASER being sold to India in 1965 and the other three being sold to Iran in 1968.

In 1983 I met Ronald French of Consett, a retired sea-going Clan Line Chief Engineer who regaled me with stories of the 'S' class and others sailing up and down in the heat off the East Coast of Africa, stories that I have worked in to the historical narrative. Since then I have uncovered the rest of the Cayzer-Clan story and compiled a full fleet list of every vessel owned by this major British liner service company. Houston Line and Scottish Line tonnage is not included, since it is considered more proper to histories of those companies. I offer this book as a testimony and tribute to the bravery, endurance and skill of Clan Line seafarers, who sometimes had to face incredible hardship and danger and also to the skill and workmanship of Clydeside and North-East Coast ship-builders. I hope that readers will judge it to be worthy of them.

Norman L. Middlemiss,

Newcastle-upon-Tyne.

December 1987.

2. EARLY DAYS.

Charles Cayzer was born on 15th July, 1843 at Hackney, London to Charles William and Mary Cayzer. His father originated from Heathersleigh, Devon, became a schoolmaster and obtained a teaching post at Poplar, London. Charles had two older and five younger sisters, four of which died in successive years of tuberculosis, none more than a few months old, and two other sisters died later from the same disease. Charles grew up beside the Thames with its busy waterfront and at 15 years of age he obtained a position as the master's clerk in a sailing ship, and set sail from the Thames bound for Japan via Bombay. He liked Bombay so much that in 1861, at the age of 17, he started work in the offices of William Nicol & Co., who in the following year became the Bombay agents of William Mackinnon's new British India Company. He thus became familiar with the British India office procedures and the Indian trade, which was to stand him in good stead later. He met Agnes Elizabeth Trickey from Clifton, Bristol, in Bombay and they married on 16th May, 1868. In April, 1873 he sailed home to England to join his wife and children, and while on extended leave of 9 months the concept of a steamship company with a direct sea link between Bombay and the two great western seaports of Britain, Liverpool and Glasgow via the Suez Canal, which had opened in 1869, began to take shape. He returned to India, resigned from British India and arrived back in Cardiff, where his family had settled, on 7th October, 1874.

The first steamer to reach Bombay and Calcutta had been the ENTERPRISE of 470 tons and 120 hp as long ago as 1825, taking 103 days steaming and 10 days refuelling time. Since then improvements in size, speed, power, reliability and bunkering arrangements aided by a Revision of the Tonnage law in 1854, which had previously discriminated against the steamship, allowed steamers to give shippers a set timetable for the arrival of goods. On the long trade routes out to India and the Far East the sailing ship remained supreme until the 1870s when the competition between sail and steam then became intense. Charles first worked for the British India agency of Grey, Dawes & Co. in London before becoming a partner in Rudstad & Cayzer in 1877, in Liverpool and then setting up a business of his own in Liverpool with a staff of 1 and buying control of a wooden barque, the 27 year old JALAWAR of 635 tons, which he traded to Bombay, making excellent profits. He then acquired the full-rigged NORTH STAR of 818 tons, which was also successful and his family moved up to Walton Park, Liverpool. An approach was then made in early 1878 to Alexander Stephen at his Linthouse, Glasgow shipyard for help in setting up a new shipping line. Stephen was prepared to invest in a new company because his shipyard was desperately short of work, and orders for two iron screw steamers of dimensions 286.0 x 34.6 x 24.0 feet were signed on 25th February, 1878 at the low price of £34,000 each, payments being cash for one third of the cost of each vessel while being built, with Alexander Stephen financing the other two thirds by Bills of Exchange which were to be redeemed within three years. John Muir, later Sir John Muir, Provost of Glasgow, of James Finlay & Company was also associated with the venture. Charles, at the age of 35, was thus able to set up a partnership with Captain Alexander Irvine, a former British India master and a long-standing friend whom he had first met in Bombay some years before. Irvine was to look after the office in Liverpool and the new company of Cayzer, Irvine & Co. began to trade at 3, Old Church Yard, Liverpool in th first week of March, 1878. Charles then drafted a long circular to the public and his friends who might be interested in his new company, for which he had to raise £22,000, on the usual 64th shares per ship basis at £560 each. In six weeks he had the money and he appointed agents in Glasgow (Turnbull & Martin), Liverpool and Manchester (Gellatly, Hankey & Sewell), London (J. & R. Grant), Cardiff (Tellefsen, Wills), Colombo (Aitken, Spence & Co.), Madras (Gordon, Woodroffe & Co.), Cape Town (James Searight & Co.) and Bombay (Finlay, Muir). Freights were not to be the responsibility of the master as per usual custom, but of the appointed agents, leaving the masters with the supervisory tasks of accepting and checking cargo.

CLAN ALPINE was launched in September, 1878 and her first trial trip was a festive occasion with 100 guests and press aboard on Tuesday 15th October, 1878. An average speed of 11 knots was obtained on 6 runs over the measured mile. She then loaded a cargo of iron railway chairs at Glasgow and sailed to Liverpool to complete her loading. At 11 p.m. on 26th October, 1878 she sailed for Bombay under the command of Capt. George Cawley R.N.R., the masters of all the early ships being officers in the Royal Navy Reserve. CLAN FRASER, the second ship, sailed from Liverpool on 23rd November, 1878, by which time orders for two more steamers from Alexander Stephen and two from Archibald McMillan of Dumbarton had been signed, completing the six Charles thought necessary for the Bombay service. The ships were of 2,900 deadweight tons, and were powered with surface-condensing, compound engines of 280 hp designed to give an average speed under loaded conditions of about 10 knots. The boilers were large for the time and had a working pressure of 80 pounds. They had two masts and were brig-rigged with an impressive array of canvas. The accommodation for 36 passengers was in a deckhouse 'fitted with every requisite to ensure their comfort in tropical as well as cold climes', with staterooms on the upper deck. They carried a surgeon and a stewardess and the first class passage to Bombay cost 25 guineas. Spacious 2 berth cabins were reserved for married couples, or for one passenger paying fare and a half. Reduced rates were granted for families, missionaries, railway employees and European and native servants. Children over 12 years of age paid full fare, between 3 and 12 years half fare, and one child under 3 years went free, if with parents. Passage included bedding, linen and cabin furniture. Wines or spirits were to be taken on board for own consumption by passengers. Every passenger was allowed 40 cu ft of baggage free, servants and children receiving half that allowance. Officers and crew were also berthed on deck, and those engaged by Charles proved to be honest and loyal, and the shore administration being very efficient the company began to make profits.

An analysis of the expenses of the early voyages is given:

Liverpool-Bombay-Liverpool in 1878.

Wages	£ 817
Provisions	£ 565
Fuel	£1110
Marine & engineers stores	£ 750
Stevedores & port charges, Liverpool and Bombay	£1045
Canal dues	£1700
Insurance	£ 768
Advertising, agents commission	£ 465
Management & office expenses	£ 232
Miscellaneous	£ 30
	£7482

The canal dues were thus half as much again as the fuel, or twice the wages of the crew. As managing owners, Cayzer, Irvine & Co. took a management charge of 2.5% of gross earnings as well as profits (or losses) as shareholders. Unlike most other managing owners, Charles also charged a commission of 5% of net profits, thereby giving an incentive to everyone to cut down costs to enable the net result to be profit rather than loss. His family, which now comprised 6 sons and 3 daughters now moved to Glasgow. 1879 did not start auspiciously for the company with a harsh blow being dealt on 27th January of the death of his new partner, Alexander Irvine at the age of 44 as the result of a heart attack. After an association of less that a year, Irvine was no longer to figure in the annals of the Clan Line, however Charles carried out his responsibilities to the widow and 3 children. He never altered the company name, even although he took another Liverpool partner, R. A. Cruikshank, who stayed with him for 7 years.

3. PERIOD OF EXPANSION.

In 1881 regular services were started to Colombo, Madras and Calcutta. Trade in South Africa was commenced with the sailing of CLAN LAMONT in September 1881, reaching Cape Town on 8th October, 1881, with crowds gathering to meet her. She was followed by CLANs GORDON, FRASER, MACLEOD, RANALD, STUART, MACKAY and CAMERON which reached Cape Town by May 1882. Trade was gradually expanded to include Delagoa Bay (Lourenco Marques), Beira and Mauritius. The Clan Line Association came into being in 1881 and was an association with several rich, influential Scottish merchants, and credits were obtained with banks for £720,000 and Alexander Stephen was promised cash and not the redemption of long-term bills for future ships. Three iron barques were purchased from G. Smith & Sons, Glasgow at a total price of £75,750 and renamed CLAN MACLEOD, CLAN MACDUFF and CLAN MACLEAN, and a vessel named MURIEL being built on the Tyne was purchased for £35,750 and renamed CLAN MURRAY. A larger office was opened at 109, Hope Street, Glasgow for the increased staff of the Association. Only one of the three iron barques was to serve the company for any length of time. CLAN MACLEOD was sold to R. M. Sloman of Hamburg in 1883 in part exchange for the Stephen built PROCIDA which was renamed CLAN GRANT. CLAN MACDUFF foundered 40 miles south of Cork Harbour on 21st October, 1881, when 32 lives were lost including the master.

At the end of 1881, a substantial building programme of 17 new ships was embarked upon starting with CLAN MONROE and CLAN MACKAY, both just under 2200 gross tons and built by Bartram, Haswell & Co. Ltd, Sunderland. All these steamers had two decks and can be divided into three classes:-

1. CLAN BUCHANAN, CLAN DRUMMOND, CLAN GRAHAM, CLAN MACGREGOR, CLAN MACKENZIE and CLAN SINCLAIR all about 2950 gross tons and were built two each by A. McMillan of Dumbarton; Napier, Shanks & Bell of Glasgow; Ramage & Ferguson of Leith.

2. CLAN CAMERON, CLAN FORBES, CLAN OGILVIE and CLAN CAMPBELL all just over 2400 gross tons and were built by Alexander Stephens of Glasgow and were the first Clan Line vessels which were built not to carry passengers.

3. CLAN MATHESON, CLAN MACPHERSON, CLAN MACARTHUR and CLAN MACINTOSH, the first pair from Napier, Shanks & Bell of Glasgow and the latter pair from Scott & Co. of Greenock. This class was much bigger at around 4000 tons and were the first vessels built of steel for the company.

In addition, CLAN MACDONALD of 2642 gross tons, built by Scott & Co. of Greenock, which did not fall into these categories.

Another loss was CLAN CAMPBELL on her maiden voyage in September, 1882 when she ran aground at Mauritius and after long attempts at salvage she broke up. By the end of 1883 the fleet had expanded greatly to 26 steamers. In this year CLAN LAMONT was chartered for several pilgrim trade voyages between India and Jeddah.

Clan Line Steamers Ltd. was formed on 25th June, 1890 at a special meeting of subscribers of the new company and Charles personally held a majority of 64ths in the 13 ships of which it became the owners. Authorised capital was £500,000 in 10,000 ordinary shares of £50 each of which 5,000 were to be issued; in addition there was created the power to issue £250,000 in 5% mortgage debentures of £100 each of which £125,000 was issued. Six new steamers were now ordered, three from Alexander Stephen and three from William Doxford at Sunderland. Charles regained control of 7 ex-Association steamers and together with original set of 6 ships, now had their engines tripled by Alexander Stephen, J. Howden and D. Rowan of Glasgow.

In October, 1892, while being converted to triple expansion, CLANs MACARTHUR, MACINTOSH, MACPHERSON and MATHESON had their accommodation improved. Two staterooms were added with three cabins on bridge deck well situated for coolness and ventilation. A large new smoking room panelled in marble, a larger music room and a clear promenade of 150 feet were created on bridge deck. In 1893 a new service was started from New York to South and East Africa. At the end of 1894 a new route to the Persian Gulf was opened up by the purchase, for the total price of £63,750, of the four steamers of the Persian Gulf Steamship Company, the AMARA, TIGRIS, GORJI and SHAT-EL-ARAB, which was renamed CLAN MACRAE the following year and sold in 1899. The first three named were sold in 1895, the year in which CLAN DRUMMOND and CLAN FRASER were the first company ships to sail up the Manchester Ship Canal, with masts cut for the bridges.

On 15th June, 1895 CLAN MATHESON sailed from Tilbury on a cruise with Charles, his family, relatives and guests aboard to Kiel on the occasion of the opening of the Kiel Canal, as a direct response to the cruise of Sir Donald Currie to the same port in TANTALLON CASTLE with Mr. Gladstone aboard. At Kiel CLAN MATHESON was kept at a distance by German officials until they discovered that a Royal Navy Admiral was a member of Charles' party. They returned via Stavanger, Bergen, Kirkwall and the cruise ended at Ayr and Greenock.

The next set of six steamers were ordered from the Barrow yard of Naval Construction and Armaments Ltd., shortly after Charles had been elected Conservative M.P. for Barrow in 1892, which he continued to represent for the next 14 years, and were of the same size as the 1891 set, and were to have remarkably long careers. Two, CLAN CAMPBELL and CLAN MACKAY were to stay in service with other owners until scrapped in 1948. In 1896 trade with the Malabar Coast, Southern India, was entered at the invitation of the Chartering Coalition, an organisation that had been formed 10 years earlier by coffee growers with the object of ensuring a regular service of chartered steamers for the export of their produce. On 19th November, 1897 preference was given to the Clan Line by this organisation.

In 1897 Charles was knighted and he was aboard CLAN MACPHERSON at the Diamond Jubilee Naval Review. By the beginning of 1898, Charles had purchased the eight remaining vessels of the Clan Line Association. During the Boer War, a number of Clan Line ships were requisitioned and a great expansion of trade to South Africa took place. Clan Line ships did not have loading rights homewards and went on to Mauritius, Batavia and more frequently India in ballast before loading return cargoes of sugar, hides, tea, cotton and grain for shipment via Suez Canal.

Around 1900 the original steamers that the company had built up in the first five years of operations were being sold for further service, and they were being replaced by the 'Turret' steamers, the first of which was delivered in 1897. They were built to take advantage of loose wording of payment clauses for Suez Canal dues, which were based entirely on deck area calculations. The Turrets had very narrow decks superimposed on a hull of normal proportions and thus secured advantageous calculation of dues. The serious shortcoming of the design was the stability at large angles of roll. The loss of buoyancy at the vessel's side and deck gave them a lesser ability to withstand rolling forces, although the full range of stability in degrees was as good as any contemporaries. While the vulnerable hatch covers were well above the waterline, care still had to be taken when loading the ship with a full cargo, to ensure that the centre of gravity was kept low.

IMPERIALIST and BULLIONIST were purchased from Angier Brothers, London in 1896 and operated on a year's trial to discover their capabilities. Charles was well satisfied with their performance and placed an order for five ships of a much larger size than previously built. CLAN MACDONALD appeared first in 1897 with two decks while CLAN BUCHANAN of 1907, the last of 30 built for the company, had three decks. All, except CLAN CUMMING and CLAN FERGUSON, which were built under licence by Vickers and Maxim, Barrow, were constructed at the Sunderland yard of William Doxford. The Turret ship came to be regarded as the mark of a Clan Line ship, however two capsized and sank on Clan Line service. CLAN RANALD under the command of Capt. Arthur Gladstone and completed in 1900, loaded 6,500 tons of grain and flour in Adelaide and in addition had about 70 tons of bunker coal on the turret deck - 50 on the starboard side and 20 to port - as well as 50 tons on the fiddley deck. She sailed at 7 a.m on 31st January, 1909 with a strong SSE wind blowing and a starboard list of four degrees which increased to six. At 2 p.m. that afternoon when off Edithburg, she suddenly heeled over further to starboard putting the turret deck under water. She stayed like this till 5 p.m. when the helm was put over to head for shore. At 8 p.m. when about 2 miles off shore the anchor was let go and 90 fathoms of cable were paid out. The ship stopped and lay head-on to a moderate wind and sea. But she continued to heel over and at 10 p.m. she capsized and sank. There was a Board of Trade Enquiry following the capsizing of the CLAN RANALD on 31st January, 1909 and the Doxfords examined in great detail the stability of all the Turrets they had built. Following this they issued special loading instructions to the owners, drawing attention to such matters as the necessity of putting water ballast into double bottom tanks if loaded down to the load line with a bulk cargo that filled the turret spaces, or if bunker fuel was being carried on the turret deck.

The loss of the CLAN GORDON in 1919 off North Carolina was blamed by the Board of Trade Enquiry on the master, who had allegedly contravened these loading instructions. CLAN GORDON, also completed in 1900, had left New York on 28th July, 1919 with case oil and bags of wax for North China ports via the Panama Canal. When clear of land her master tested the ship's stability by putting the helm over each way with no resultant heeling. Two days later in the morning, he decided to pump out the water in Nos. 1 and 2 double bottom ballast tanks. This would put the ship down a little by the stern to give the propeller better power in the water and so increase speed, and also in the mistaken belief that this would improve her bad weather behaviour. During the afternoon the ship took a list of five degrees, but worse followed at 4-30 p.m. when the helm was put over to port to swing the ship for sun bearings and the ship heeled right over and capsized. There was no time to launch the boats and the crew walked along the side of the ship and on to her bottom, where they sat on the upturned keel until they were rescued. CLAN GORDON floated upside down for some time before sinking.

In 1901 the Assam-Bengal Railway was completed and the jetties at Chittagong to the east of Calcutta were opened. Clan Line inaugurated sailings from that port for tea and jute, CLAN MENZIES taking the first cargo in July, 1901. In the last six months of 1903, 15 CLANs loaded at Chittagong.

Cayzer Irvine & Co. was incorporated into a limited company on 1st July, 1907. Authorised capital was £1,000,000 consisting of 5,000 5% cumulative Preference shares of £100 and 5,000 Ordinary shares of £100 each. 4,000 Preference shares and 3,000 Ordinary shares were issued all of which, except 6 Ordinary shares, were allotted to Sir Charles. The other six went to the other directors i.e. his 4 eldest sons and his 2 sons-in-law. The business of Cayzer, Irvine & Co. was acquired for £700,000 by Cayzer, Irvine & Co. Ltd. Sir Charles' second eldest son John, tragically died in 1908 and his fourth eldest son Arthur, died after a long illness in June, 1909. His eldest son Charles William, retired early from the business in 1910 after a long series of disagreements with his father.

There were other ships constructed for the company during the Turret building programme and one of these, CLAN MACINTYRE completed in 1903 by Furness, Withy & Co. at their West Hartlepool yard, was the last ship to sight the cargo-liner WARATAH with 211 people aboard, 8 hours out from Durban on 27th July, 1909. They exchanged signals and remained in sight for three hours, and then the WARATAH disappeared without trace. The end must have been sudden and she was not equipped with radio, which at that time was still a fairly recent development.

The Turret CLAN CAMERON, built in 1900, loaded at Birkenhead in 1909 a heavy boiler for Tuticorin by floating crane into her No. 2 tween deck. There was no crane at Tuticorin capable of lifting it, so it was decided to drop it from the harbour deck of the Turret into the water and float it to the shore. The boiler had previously been tested for buoyancy by floating it in Birkenhead dock. CLAN CAMERON then voyaged to Bombay, where the nearest suitable crane lifted it out of her hold and onto the harbour deck and she set sail for Tuticorin. On arrival, a lunch was arranged and the boiler was to be ceremoniously dropped into the harbour after lunch. The party of representatives, well fortified after a good lunch, assembled on the lower bridge to watch, and the mate wielding a polished lifeboat axe, cut through the single 4" manilla rope holding the boiler. It plunged with a big splash into the water, bobbed up and down a bit and then settled and promptly sank! The incredulous expressions on the faces of the luncheon party told it all - they just couldn't believe it! The explanation was simple: the floating of the boiler in the dock at Birkenhead had swelled the wooden plugs of the numerous inlet and outlet openings and in the subsequent six weeks of hot, dry weather they had dried out, and after the first big plug had fallen out when the boiler hit the water, the others blew out as the water entered and compressed the air. The boiler lies to this day on the bottom of the harbour at Tuticorin. Needless to say this method of unloading heavy lifts was discontinued.

CLAN MACLAREN of 1899 under the command of Capt. George Shearer voyaged to New Zealand in 1909 and rounded the Horn. She went outward to South Africa and then onto Bunbury for orders and was instructed to load a cargo of coal at Port Kembla, Queensland for Wellington. She doubled back for a cargo of concentrates to stiffen her bottom at Port Pirie before loading wool at Auckland, Gisborne, Napier, Picton, Lyttleton, Timaru, Omaru, Port Chalmers and Wellington. They left Wellington with a freeboard of 3 feet 4 inches and open gangways opposite the hatchways on the main deck, and soon after ran into a severe gale and lost 30 tons of coal and 10 sheep washed overboard from the deck. Lifelines were essential to moving around on deck. When the wind was favourable, trysails and staysails were set during the 6,000 mile run to the Horn. Safely round they arrived in Surrey Commercial Dock on their 62nd day out and turned out an excellent cargo.

Her sister CLAN MACFADYEN of 1899 had an unusual voyage in 1911 when after discharge at Cape Town and East London she proceeded to Ananalava and Majunga in Madagascar to load mangrove bark from dhows at open beaches. A cable was then received from Head Office to proceed to position 17°5'S 38°30'E to pick up 900 tons of bark stacked on the beach near the mouth of the Moebozi river. Capt. Mason knew this coast well and wisely went first to Quelimane to ask about this river mouth and then anchored four miles off the coast at the indicated position and sent the ship's boat to see if there was sufficient draft at the Bar. At high water it was soon found that there was only 12 to 15 feet depth of water, with CLAN MACFADYEN drawing 19 feet. Unfortunately, the ship's boat grounded and overturned during this process, but natives soon had the boat righted and launched to return to the ship. CLAN MACFADYEN then went back to Quelimane to cable for instructions and was ordered to rendez-vous with CLAN ALPINE, a Turret built in 1899, and transfer 2,000 tons of bark into her holds. CLAN MACFADYEN then proceeded to Chittagong to load jute and tea for London.

Her sister CLAN MACKINNON homeward-bound from Savannah, Georgia with a mixed cargo for Glasgow under the command of Capt. H. R. East, rescued the entire crew of the Norwegian cutter ELSIE in 1910 in difficulties in extremely rough weather. After the rescue, CLAN MACKINNON was hove-to for several hours in deteriorating weather. The Norwegian Government presented a cup to Capt. East in appreciation of his efforts.

Furness, Withy managed two ships that had been built in 1907 at their West Hartlepool yard for the Chesapeake & Ohio Steamship Company Ltd. RAPIDAN and ROANOKE were then purchased by the company the following year to become CLAN MACIVER and CLAN MACINNES respectively, but were sold back to Furness, Withy in 1914, resuming their former names. CLAN MACGILLIVRAY, completed in 1911 by Armstrong, Whitworth at their Walker, Newcastle yard, gave the longest service of any vessel owned by the company. She served as a hospital ship for the Anzac landing in Gallipoli in 1915. She survived two World Wars and was still able to give a few more years service before being scrapped in 1949. CLAN MACRAE and CLAN DAVIDSON, built in 1912 by William Doxford & Sons Ltd. at Sunderland, were the first Clan Line vessels to be fitted with refrigerating machines and were specially equipped for the Australian homeward trade. They had a service speed of 14 knots and averaged 31 days for the voyage from Western Australia to Europe and had three refrigerated sisters, CLAN MACARTHUR, CLAN MACEWEN, and CLAN MACTAVISH, all with a capacity of 3,500 tons of refrigerated cargo in addition to general cargo. CLAN MACQUARRIE of 1913, a shelter-deck vessel was the last ship to be built at Linthouse, Govan for the Clan Line by Alexander Stephen & Sons Ltd., the shipyard that financially supported the company in the early days. CLAN MACQUARRIE was one of five fine new vessels completed for the company in the year before the Great War, including one that was purchased while fitting out on the Tyne for J. & C. Harrison Ltd., London as HARFLETE. Tragically two of them, CLAN MACTAVISH and CLAN MACCORQUODALE were not to be afloat at the end of the war.

4. 'SCOTS NAVY' IN ACTION.

CLAN ROSS of 1914 was one of three vessels to have cruiser sterns, at that time a new development, the other two being CLAN OGILVY and CLAN CAMPBELL. However, subsequent vessels revert to the traditional counter sterns until the group of vessels constructed by Ayrshire Dockyard at Irvine appeared in 1920. CLAN ROSS survived torpedoing in the first World War, and bombing in the Bay of Biscay in 1940, but succumbed to another torpedo in 1942, 350 miles south west of Bombay. Sadly Sir Charles died at his favourite Scottish estate of Gartmore near Aberfoyle on Thursday, 28th September, 1916 and his third son August became Chairman, Herbert became Vice-Chairman and Harold joined the company when the war was over. It is coincidental that his close friend, Sir William Theodore Doxford, died in the same week at Grindon Hall, Sunderland. The two had collaborated over the Turret building programme and on experiments with marine diesel engines. Sir Charles was 73 years of age and the company owned 60 ships at the time of his death, but by the end of the war, had lost 28 ships to enemy action and marine hazard. The silent, unseen enemy of the submarine torpedo had accounted for 19 ships, three were sunk by collision, one was wrecked, one by mine, and one, CLAN MACNAUGHTON foundered in the North Atlantic while serving as an Armed Merchant Cruiser in 1915. CLAN CHISHOLM was luckier than most, being attacked by gunfire from submarine on no less than three occasions, but managed to escape each time. Two, CLAN MATHESON and CLAN GRANT were sunk by the German cruiser EMDEN, and CLAN MACTAVISH was sunk by the raider MOEWE. As a result of these actions, the ships became known as 'The Fighting Clans'.

CLAN MACTAVISH was carrying a valuable cargo of leather, wool, rubber and other war materials home from Australia when MOEWE caught up with her as dusk was falling on 16th January, 1916, 120 miles south west of Funchal, Maderia. Capt. Donna-Schlodien of MOEWE sent a radio message to try to find out the identity of the vessel before she escaped into the night. Capt. Oliver of CLAN MACTAVISH unwittingly gave this away when Donna-Schlodien lied that he was the Harrison ship AUTHOR, bound from Liverpool to Port Natal, which he had sunk three days earlier. Capt. Oliver was ordered to stop, but tried desperately to escape in the darkness by ordering full ahead. After the customary shot across the bow, CLAN MACTAVISH started using her radio and MOEWE sent two shells across at a range of 300 metres, aimed at the radio station. CLAN MACTAVISH replied by sending shells from her small 57mm gun over MOEWE's bridge, and the surprised Donna-Schlodien began rapid fire with shell after shell hitting home. Capt. Oliver was a brave adversary and he kept up the action long after it was apparent that they were out-gunned and out-aimed with no chance of winning and not much chance of surviving if he continued to fight. The Indian crew panicked and tried to get into one of the ship's boats to escape. A shell from MOEWE was put into the middle of this crowd, sending bodies flying and killing 18 Indians. A fire broke out and Capt. Oliver gave up the fight by signalling he had stopped firing. CLAN MACTAVISH was seriously damaged with hissing steam escaping from the main boiler and her valuable cargo would soon have been lost. Donna-Schlodien was annoyed when CLAN MACTAVISH sank two hours after the beginning of the fight before he could trans-ship the rubber. Capt. Oliver was brought to the bridge of the MOEWE and reprimanded for having fought back, when he could so easily have surrendered and saved lives. He stood his ground firmly, replying he thought he was in battle with an armed merchant ship and expected he could at least hold his own. He had specific orders that nothing short of disaster was to prevent his delivering the cargo to England and if he had to do it over again he would do exactly the same.

The German cruiser EMDEN had slipped out of Tsingtao, China on the declaration of war on 5th August, 1914 and headed for the Guam area of the Pacific before voyaging through the Dutch East Indies and entering the Bay of Bengal on 9th

September. There she started her raiding, and on 14th September Capt. Harris of CLAN MATHESON heard and saw the plume of smoke from the destruction of the British steamer TRABBOCH. The coal dust in her holds had ignited when the explosive charges set to sink her had gone off and a big column of flame tinged with blue, shot up into the air. Capt. Harris headed off to the east, but the EMDEN caught up with him later in the day. He did not stop, even after blank rounds had been fired followed by blasts from the EMDEN's foghorn. However, after a live round set up a large fountain of water before the bow of CLAN MATHESON he did finally heave to. The valuable cargo included locomotives, cars, typewriters and other expensive machines and one fine race horse. CLAN MATHESON sank within thirty minutes after explosive charges went off and became the first casualty of the Clan Line in WW1. Next day the crew were transferred to the neutral Norwegian steamer DOVRE.

On 15th October CLAN GRANT, a Turret vessel, was spotted by the enemy just before midnight heading west towards Minicoy Island, well known in the Maldives for its great lighthouse. Capt. Leslie was ordered to follow the EMDEN during the night after a prize crew had been sent across. At daybreak the ship was searched, and she was found to be carrying 4,000 tons of mixed cargo including live cattle, a large stock of beer and cigarettes and engine oil and several hours were spent transferring these and other items including crockery, table linen, soldering irons and fire bricks for the boilers. CLAN GRANT was then sunk by gunfire and the crew were transferred to the German collier BURESK and then to the captured British steamer ST. EGBERT which was ordered to Cochin arriving on 20th October. EMDEN was finally destroyed in the fierce battle with H.M.A.S. SYDNEY off the Cocos Islands on 9th November, 1914 and was run aground.

At the outbreak of war the fleet stood at 56 fine steamers of one quarter of a million gross tons and although half of them were destroyed, they were all replaced during the war by more modern, speedier vessels. Shortly after the outbreak, CLAN MACMILLAN under the command of Capt. G. Young and CLAN MACPHEE under Capt. Oliver and CLAN MACFAYDEN under Capt. Miller, became troop transports for the South African Union Expeditionary Force. The transports assembled at Luderitz, south of Walvis Bay, where there was unfortunately no fresh water, so CLAN MACMILLAN with her deep tank, was frequently employed in water trips to Cape Town for the troops before the transports departed en-masse for Europe.

During the hunt for the German cruiser KÖNIGSBERG in September, 1914, CLAN MACRAE built in 1912, aided the survivors of H.M.S. PEGASUS which had been sunk by the KÖNIGSBERG. The cruiser went on to sink one more vessel, the Ellerman Line CITY OF WINCHESTER, before she took refuge seven miles up the Rufiji delta, south of Dar-Es-Salaam, where she was located by the hunters in October, 1914. There then followed a nine month seige before KÖNIGSBERG was finally sunk in July, 1915 by the two monitors SEVERN and MERSEY, which were specially sent out from England. CLAN MACRAE went on to tow H.M.S. CHATHAM one of the hunters, off the Leven Rocks near Kilindini, Mombasa later in 1914.

CLAN MACGILLIVRAY, built on the Tyne in 1911, served as a hospital ship throughout the Gallipoli campaign in the Dardanelles in 1915. She took off many wounded from the beaches at Suvla Bay between 9th and 11th August, 1915 in company with the prize SÜDMARK which became the fourth CLAN MACKAY in 1921.

CLAN MACALISTER built on the Clyde in 1903, became the first company vessel to be torpedoed and sunk when she was hit by U35 some 120 miles from Cape Martello, Crete, on 6th November, 1915 on a voyage from Liverpool to Calcutta with general cargo. Two others, CLAN MACLEOD and CLAN MACFARLANE, quickly followed her fate in the Mediterranean during the following month. There was an ugly incident, long remembered by seafarers, after CLAN MACLEOD was torpedoed 100 miles E.S.E. from Malta when the crew were ruthlessly machine-gunned when abandoning ship by U33 commander Gansser, killing 12 and wounding many others. Gansser had closely followed CLAN MACLEOD for two hours, preventing the crew from lowering the lifeboats until the ship sank beneath them.

By the middle of 1917 all Clan Line vessels were sailing in convoy to and from India and South Africa and CLAN MACPHERSON built in 1905, loaded 12,000 tons of Egyptian cotton for Boston and joined a homeward convoy from Alexandria on 3rd December, 1917. They safely transitted the Mediterranean and CLAN MACPHERSON detached from the convoy midway during the Gibraltar to U.K. last lap and reached Boston safely. One for whom the convoy system came too late, was the Turret CLAN ALPINE, which was torpedoed and sunk by U60 while sailing alone 40 miles from Muckle Flugga, North Shetlands, having left the Tyne on 7th June, 1917 for the White Sea, to load a cargo of timber. CLAN MACKAY and CLAN MATHESON both built in 1917, were sunk by collision within twelve days of each other in May, 1918. The former was sunk 520 miles S.W. from the Scillies while homeward bound from Calcutta, while the latter sank about 450 miles S.E. of Cape Race while homeward bound from New Orleans and New York with barley, oats and steel. CLAN MACVEY had the shortest career of any Clan Line vessel when she sank on her maiden voyage 5 miles to the west of the Needles on 8th August, 1918. She had sailed from the Tyne, the river of her birth, with coal for Port Said two days before and had been missed by a torpedo, probably from the same submarine, the day before she was hit half a mile S.E. of Anvil Point near Swanage.

CLAN MACNEIL, another Turret vessel, became the last company ship lost in WW1 when she was torpedoed and sunk on 6th August, 1918 by the submarine UC34 10 miles N. of Alexandria on a voyage from Karachi to Marseilles with grain and onions. No fewer than five vessels were torpedoed and sunk in the Mediterranean during the last year of the war, the others being CLANs FORBES, MACDOUGALL, MACPHERSON and MACCORQUODALE. In 1918 the company acquired Scottish Shire Line with refrigerated meat services to Australia/New Zealand from Sir James Caird for £750,000 and also acquired Houston Line with similar services to South America as well as South and East Africa for £4M just prior to Armistice. Clan Line were looking for spare tonnage to fill the gaps in their fleet until new ships could be built and the Houston Line services fitted in well with their own. Robert P. Houston, the founder, thus sold out to one of the chief members of the Conference which had fought to keep him out of the South African trade. Sir Charles of course never saw this for he died two years earlier.

5. INTER-WAR YEARS.

The funnel colours of the Houston vessels remained red with a black top during the twenties, the only exception being that the Clan Line house flag was flown at the foremast while the Houston flag flew on the mainmast. During the thirties however, the Houston ships wore half-Clan, half-Houston funnel colours by painting the famous twin red bands on the black portion, which was extended down the funnel. The funnel colours of the Scottish Shire Line vessels remained yellow. In 1920-21, CLAN MACBEOLAN, CLAN MACEWEN and CLAN MACRAE were transferred to the British and South American Steam Navigation Company Ltd. with Houston Line as managers and renamed HALESIUS, BUTESHIRE and BANFFSHIRE respectively. At the same time CLAN MACARTHUR was transferred to the Scottish Shire Line and renamed BERWICKSHIRE. CLAN SKENE and CLAN KEITH were also transferred at this time to the British and South American Steam Navigation Company Ltd. becoming HALOCRATES and HILARIUS respectively, but were transferred back to Cayzer, Irvine & Co. Ltd. in 1924 resuming their former names.

After the war Clan Line were extended loading rights homewards from South Africa particularly for the export of fruit and as well as accelerating their own building programme to replace the enormous losses, the company purchased two vessels from Lang & Fulton Ltd., the ARDGRYFE and ARDGARROCH and renamed them CLAN KENNETH and CLAN KENNEDY respectively. Also purchased was the HUNTSCRAFT from Harris & Dixon Ltd., being renamed CLAN MACKAY a year later. This vessel, completed in July, 1913 for German owners by William Doxford & Sons Ltd. as SÜDMARK, had been captured and requisitioned by the Admiralty and managed by Harris & Dixon Ltd. until 1917 when they bought her. Another purchase for the British and South American Steam Navigation Co. Ltd. at this time was the Belgian vessel YPRESVILLE, built at Glasgow in 1918 for Lloyd Royal Belge. She was renamed HALIZONES, and was brought back into the ownership of Cayzer, Irvine & Co. Ltd. in 1923 and renamed CLAN MACWHIRTER after a three year spell as the WILLCASINO with the Convoy S.S. Co. Ltd. Twelve vessels were completed for the company between 1920 and 1924, eight by Ayrshire Dockyard at Irvine, three by Lithgows at Port Glasgow and one, CLAN MACILWRAITH of 1924, by Greenock Dockyard, which had been purchased by the company in 1918. These were the last company vessels to be issued with a set of sails.

The company ventured into another area of trading in 1926 when they bought two small steamers, formerly the Navy store ships POLYANTHUS and IVY, for St. Lawrence trading from Mexican owners and registered them in Montreal. The NAYARIT was kept for only two years before being sold, whereas the COLIMA served the company until 1930 when she was sold to British Trade Crusades, for whom she gave another three years service. The company replaced COLIMA with the SINALOA and she continued St. Lawrence trading until sold in 1933 to Greeks. As trading conditions got worse the company got rid of any trade, such as those to the River Plate in 1926, which was sold to Kaye, Son & Co. Ltd., London, and on the St. Lawrence which did not fit into the main pattern of trading. All vessels were maintained on the high seas during the depression, although in 1926 and again in 1932 the company capital was reconstructed. The company had only four new-buildings between 1924 and 1936 but two of these, CLAN MACDONALD of 1928 and CLAN MACDOUGALL of 1929 had revolutionary engines. They had Burmeister & Wain double acting four stroke air injection diesel engines with electric pressure-charging blowers. They were the first company ships to have composite superstructures and long foredecks and were fitted with a 120 ton derrick on the foremast. However, CLAN MACPHERSON of 1929 and CLAN MACALISTER of 1930 reverted to triple expansion engines, but for the first time working in conjunction with the Bauer-Wach exhaust turbine. So satisfactory did the experiment prove that many of the older ships of the company were converted to this system. All four vessels were built by Greenock Dockyard.

When CLAN MACBRIDE of 1912 departed for India under the command of Capt. Last in December, 1931 fully loaded with cargo, there were eight fine racehorses stowed next to the poop on either side of No. 5 hatch. Things went well until they were in the Mediterranean, but by Christmas day a full gale had blown up and the horses were in a sorry state, being wet and frightened. H.S. Pengelly, later Capt., forfeited his Christmas dinner and volunteered to move the horses onto No. 5 hatch, and the horses were landed in Bombay in fine condition. A more unusual cargo awaited them. Forty boxes of bullion containing bar gold and hundreds of thousands of British gold sovereigns were on the manifest for shipment to Tilbury. These were locked in the only high security place in the ship - the Chief Steward's store which had iron bulkheads all round and a heavy iron door with a good lock, and arrived safe and sound.

The opportunity was taken to purchase five second-hand ships from companies who had not been so fortunate. These were two standard WW1 types purchased from White Star Line for £53,000 each in 1933 and which had been used on the Australian run, renaming them CLAN COLQUHOUN and CLAN FARQUHAR, and two purchased from C. W. Kellock & Co. Ltd. in 1929, renaming them CLAN GRAHAM and CLAN GRANT, and CLAN ROBERTSON purchased for the New Zealand Shipping Co. Ltd. in 1934 as the OTAKI and sold to Stanhope S.S. Co. in 1938. In 1932 the ARGYLLSHIRE of 1911 was transferred from the Scottish Shire Line to become CLAN URQUHART. She had five masts, three of them being before the funnel and two aft. She was one of the largest vessels to go up the Manchester Ship Canal, her length being 526 feet and she was one of three sisters. SHROPSHIRE and WILTSHIRE, which was wrecked in 1922, were however owned by the Federal Steam Navigation Company Ltd. SHROPSHIRE was transferred to the New Zealand Shipping Co. Ltd. in 1921 and while refitting at Falmouth late in 1921 she was badly damaged by fire and was sent to London for conversion into a passenger liner with accommodation for 400 people in two classes. She sailed to New Zealand from March, 1923 until torpedoed and sunk on 11th December, 1940, 110 miles west of St. Kilda. In October, 1933 CLAN BUCHANAN, CLAN SINCLAIR and CLAN KENNETH were sold for the combined price of £15,000 to Hughes, Bolckow & Co. Ltd. for demolition at Blyth.

The sons of Sir Charles achieved their aim of the largest purely cargo-carrying concern in the world in the late thirties, with a combined total of 400,000 gross tons of the Clan Line, Scottish Shire Line and Houston Line. The big CLAN MACARTHUR and CLAN MACAULAY and PERTHSHIRE of the associated Scottish Shire Line signalled the start of a big building programme in 1936 by Greenock Dockyard of six cylinder triple expansion steamers fitted with low pressure exhaust turbines. The ships had twin propellers to maintain the fast service speed of 17 knots. CLAN CAMERON, completed in February, 1937, was 14 feet shorter and three feet less in beam with dimensions 463.7 x 63.0 x 29.9 feet and was the lead ship of a class of 20 very similar ships constructed for, or managed by, the company in the late thirties and throughout the war, ending with CLAN CUMMING of 1946. Moreover, they were shelter-deckers and so their gross tonnages were 3,000 tons less than that of the original trio. Improvements and alterations were made during the building of the class, so that no more than four ships were completely identical.

The first sub-group of the class included CLAN CAMERON as well as CLANs CAMPBELL, CHISHOLM, CHATTAN, CUMMING, BUCHANAN and FERGUSON, of which the first four were exactly identical, with the others differing in minor details only. They were magnificent ships of heavily-built sturdy appearance with imposing bridges, large funnels and heavy derrick gear. The midships bridge deck was separated by a hatchway from the bridge structure, which was comparatively short and four decks high, plated in over the two lower decks in the first five ships. They had a long forecastle and short poop with reasonably good sheer. An 80-ton derrick was abaft the mainmast and three other heavy derricks were fitted, along with three sets of derrick posts and a stump mast at the aft end of the bridge deck. The 'tween decks were high and hatchways large for the carriage of awkward sized loads. Next came four nearly identical ships CLANs FRASER, FORBES, LAMONT and MENZIES with an extra house and boat deck above the bridge deck. The remaining ships of the class constructed during the war differed little from CLAN FRASER. However, CLAN MACDONALD of 1939, which received the name of the first Turret ship and also of the first motor ship, and CLAN MACDOUGALL of 1944, were exceptions, being slightly larger and fitted with two ten cylinder diesel engines.

6. 'SCOTS NAVY' IN ACTION AGAIN.

Three of the CLAN CAMERON class steamers were requisitioned by the Admiralty while still on the stocks at Greenock Dockyard and were completed as H.M.S. ATHENE, H.M.S. ENGADINE and H.M.S. BONAVENTURE, the first two as seaplane depot ships. H.M.S. BONAVENTURE was commissioned into the Royal Navy on 23rd January, 1943, as a depot ship for 'X' craft midget submarines and for the next two years operated from secret hideouts on the coast of Scotland for operations against enemy-controlled Norway. On 22nd September, 1943, her midget submarines made the daring attack on the TIRPITZ in Altenfjord and she also conducted all the training for midget and human torpedoes. She carried out in total, three operations off the Norwegian coast and then her craft took part in D-Day operations. The BONAVENTURE sailed for the Pacific on 21st February, 1945, with a second flotilla of midget subs for operations against the Japanese. A few weeks before Japan surrendered they penetrated the defences of the Johore Strait and torpedoed the cruiser TAKAO. They also cut the marine cable between Singapore-Saigon-Japan, which forced the enemy to use radio which could be picked up and deciphered by the Allies. She also flew the flag of an American Admiral commanding submarines of the U.S. Seventh fleet for a while. Four Victoria Crosses, 12 D.S.O.s and 50 other awards for bravery were won by the officers and men of her flotillas. After the war had ended she was used as a Navy Transport steaming over 60,000 miles between Australia, Japan, China, Malaya and the Phillipines. She rescued 85 survivors and a dog from the frigate H.M.S. AIRE, aground on the notorious Bombay Reef, on Christmas Eve 1946. Bombay Reef lies just off the main Hong Kong-Singapore shipping lanes. In Spring of 1947 the BONAVENTURE returned home for a thorough overhaul before returning to Clan Line service early in 1948 as CLAN DAVIDSON.

In total, Clan Line lost 30 ships during World War II, of which 16 were torpedoed by submarine, 6 were bombed or hit by aerial torpedo, 3 were mined, 3 were lost by collision, one was sunk by German raider and one lost by fire and stranding. CLAN CHISHOLM was the first casualty of the war on 17th October, 1939 when two torpedoes slammed into her in the darkness 300 miles off Cape Finisterre. She had sailed independently as far as Port Said with a full cargo from India, and had joined a slow 9.5 knot convoy at Gibraltar on the last lap. After the Convoy Commodore had been sunk four days out, CLAN CHISHOLM went to full speed and headed away from the apparent area of danger, but four hours later she met the same fate. Twenty four hours later, CLAN MACBEAN from the same convoy came within 100 feet of ramming a U-boat which had surfaced and was shelling her after missing with a torpedo. There was no time for the U-boat gun crew to get below before the crash dive, and they were probably lost and CLAN MACBEAN escaped unharmed by the bold, attacking moves of her master Capt. E. Coultas. Masters of merchant ships continually under the threat of submarine torpedo cannot as a rule hit back, unless the submarine surfaces, but patiently have to avoid areas of danger or even backtrack. However, they can hit back with their guns, if they have any, at aircraft and surface ships. Herbert Cayzer who had taken the title of Lord Rotherwick in 1937, highlighted the need for equal priority to be given to supplying merchant ships with guns, in a speech on becoming President of the Chamber of Shipping in February, 1941, so that no vessel was left without means of repelling attack. The actions when Clan Line ships did hit back, mostly in the Mediterranean, are indicative of their fighting spirit. Indeed, the company was well known as the Scots Navy on account of the sleeve rings of the officers being identical to those of the Royal Navy.

On 15th November, 1940 CLAN FORBES and CLAN FRASER sailed from the Clyde in convoy with two other ships to take part in the first west to east supply convoy run to Malta since the entry of Italy into the war. CLAN FORBES had been disguised by the carpenters and fitters of the Clyde as the submarine depot ship H.M.S. MAIDSTONE with a dummy funnel. The other two ships had left by Gibraltar and on 27th November the first hostile aircraft had been dealt with by carrier fighters. At nightfall the two Clan vessels took leave of their heavy escort and made a dash through the Pantellaria Channel. During the following afternoon bombs were dropped all around the merchant ships, with CLAN FRASER being heavily straddled, but to the relief of everyone both ships entered Grand Harbour, Valletta. Four other merchant ships that had made the passage from the eastern end of the Mediterranean were already in harbour. It was a proud moment for the Clan Line for five of the six ships flew their house flag, the others being CLAN FERGUSON, CLAN MACAULAY and LANARKSHIRE of the Scottish Shire Line. Early in January, 1941, CLAN MACAULAY made another run into Malta and had a miraculous escape from destruction while in harbour. There had been a gale on the night of 17th/18th January and her master had asked next day to be moved to a new berth as his anchors had dragged. The ship was beginning to move when an air raid developed and two heavy bombs crashed into the water just where she had been moored a few minutes earlier.

CLAN MACDONALD was Convoy Commodore ship for a passage through the Mediterranean with munitions bound for Piraeus in January, 1941. She survived repeated attacks by high level and dive-bombers and was shelled as she passed through the Narrows. However, she arrived safely and discharged her valuable cargo. She then went via the Suez Canal as far as Brisbane and returned to the U.K. where an enemy bomber dropped two bombs very close to her at anchor.

CLAN FRASER arrived in Piraeus with a cargo of Military stores on 4th April, 1941, after another transit of the Mediterranean. On the evening of 6th April, she was struck by three bombs during an air raid, one landing forward, one amidships and one aft and seven crew members were killed. The remainder evacuated ship and for five hours CLAN FRASER blazed fiercely, glowing red hot from bulwarks to water-line, and then blew up with tremendous force. The explosion did enormous damage to Piraeus port and other shipping and shook buildings 15 miles inland. CLAN CUMMING was in port with CLAN FRASER having made the Mediterranean transit in convoy from Gibraltar, leaving on 6th January, 1941. She had safely sailed again from

Piraeus after discharging her valuable cargo, with a heavy escort but was torpedoed on 18th January and returned to Piraeus to dry-dock. When CLAN FRASER exploded the force sent CLAN CUMMING rolling onto her beam ends, and a steel plate measuring 23 feet x 3 feet landed on her bridge top, while half of CLAN FRASER's windlass crashed through No. 4 hatch and started a fire. Later a section of the CLAN FRASER bridge structure weighing 12.5 tons was found nearly a mile away and thirty feet of her 80 ton derrick was found in a park! On 14th April, CLAN CUMMING got a seaworthy certificate and sailed that night, shooting down a plane on the way out, but ran into a minefield and sank after a heavy explosion.

On 28th April, 1941, while on her way from Durban to Colombo, CLAN BUCHANAN was intercepted by the German surface raider PINQUIN after being sighted by the raider's aircraft. Cpt. D. Davenport Jones surrendered his ship only when the situation was hopeless, with debris from shell explosions blown into the engine-room and engines disabled. None of the crew were killed and all were safely transferred to the raider. Ten days later the raider was sunk by the cruiser CORNWALL, which picked up as many survivors as she could. In despatching this particular menace to British merchantmen on the high seas, there was a heavy loss of life among the CLAN BUCHANAN crew of over 100, with only 13 survivors.

Four Clan ships, including the managed EMPIRE SONG, were in another convoy that sailed from Gibraltar in May, 1941 for Malta. The convoy was subject to heavy air attack and on the night of 8th May, when about 45 miles west of Pantellaria EMPIRE SONG was badly damaged when she struck mines. Efforts to put the subsequent fires out were unsuccessful and internal explosions shook her as she steamed along. When the temperature in No. 1 hold had reached 110 degrees the order to abandon ship was given. A destroyer was badly damaged later during an investigation when EMPIRE SONG blew up. CLAN LAMONT, CLAN CHATTAN and CLAN CAMPBELL, the latter suffering from engine trouble, all made it safely to Malta.

In the same month on the 20th, CLAN MACQUARRIE actually rode over a submarine while zigzagging independently on her way to South Africa. Her master had spotted what looked like a tide rip travelling slowly northward about six cables ahead. He headed straight for the head of the tell-tale ripple. Five minutes later, there was a terrific impact under the foremast and the bows of the CLAN MACQUARRIE appeared to rise and for ten seconds the whole ship vibrated from whatever was under the hull. Then there were two more severe bumps, one under the deep tank amidships and the other under the mainmast. For ten seconds CLAN MACQUARRIE rode over the submarine and forced her down. Then the buoyancy of the submarine forced her up and she bumped twice more on the bottom of CLAN MACQUARRIE. The submarine was presumed sunk. After the coal had been worked out of the deep tank it was found that six frames on the port side and five on the starboard side had parted from the ship's side. The damage was quickly repaired in Cape Town.

CLAN MACDONALD arrived safely in Malta on 28th September, 1941 after narrowly missing being torpedoed in an air/sea battle during which 14 enemy aircraft were shot down. On 16th October she began a spectacular run home with 11 passengers including 4 children and passed through the Narrows by night. She then hoisted the French flag on instructions and continued on with four Italian aircraft shadowing her. By about 3 p.m. suspicions were confirmed when another three planes circled overhead, and one dropped a torpedo which missed. The second aircraft did the same, which missed only by five feet and then followed up by dropping a mine which also missed. The third aircraft was hit several times by CLAN MACDONALD's gunners and staggered and lost height and broke off. Two hours later a torpedo bomber received hits and retired badly damaged without launching torpedoes. The next day another enemy aircraft circled respectfully out of range, and CLAN MACDONALD reached GIbraltar safely on 19th October.

CLAN FERGUSON had sailed from the Clyde with 245 troops and a full cargo of war material and arrived at Malta at about the same time as CLAN

MACDONALD was leaving. She tried to get back to Gibraltar a week later unescorted, but after suffering several attacks from torpedo bombers, was ordered back to Malta. A month later she acted as a decoy to try to tempt the Italian Navy out, but they stayed in port and CLAN FERGUSON returned to Malta and loaded scrap, spending Christmas 1941 there. On Boxing Day evening she left with a small convoy bound for Alexandria and suffered above-water damage from close bombing, but reached Egypt by the New Year. She sailed in convoy back to Malta on 16th January, 1942 with 175 troops and a full cargo of explosives and foodstuffs and 1,000 tons of fuel oil and 270 tons of coal and arrived on the 19th. After discharging her cargo, she spent four days in dry-dock having her bottom cleaned. She returned to Alexandria safely having suffered continuous air attacks for the first two days out, and then returned to the U.K. via Bombay, Cape Town, New York and Halifax.

The next convoy from Alexandria was in the following month of February, when a fast four ship convoy including CLAN CHATTAN and CLAN CAMPBELL set sail on the 12th. The inevitable air attacks started and CLAN CAMPBELL received a direct hit the next day and was damaged by a near miss off Tobruk and had to be detached there. Fierce high level and low level attacks continued and CLAN CHATTAN was hit in one of her holds on the 14th and caught fire. She had to be sunk by an escort, as had the third merchantman an hour later when her engines were disabled. The fourth, BRECONSHIRE, returned to Alexandria but attempted to break through again on the 19th March in another fast four ship convoy that included the repaired CLAN CAMPBELL. The situation in Malta was now desperate with practically no food, fuel or ammunition left to hold off the continuous air attacks on the island. The convoy received the expected air attacks on the morning of the third day and involved more than 150 enemy aircraft using torpedoes and heavy bombs. All were beaten off, but in the afternoon enemy cruisers and a battleship were sighted and the convoy turned away behind a heavy smoke screen. The British cruisers accurate fire and the determination of the destroyers to close and launch torpedoes ultimately persuaded the enemy to turn away. The four merchantmen dispersed to make their own way to Malta with one British cruiser and six destroyers nearby. In spite of bad weather the enemy air attacks did not let up and CLAN CAMPBELL was only 50 miles from her destination when she was heavily attacked. In the running battle she managed to gain another 30 miles before a dive bomber scored a hit from 50 feet. Her engine room flooded and she sank soon afterwards 8 miles from the Filfola Islands and thankfully 112 survivors were picked up by a destroyer, but thirty lives were lost. Two of the other merchantmen made it to harbour, but one was scuttled as she was blazing furiously with a cargo of ammunition. The fourth, the BRECONSHIRE, was disabled by a direct hit in the engine room, and was towed to the confined Marsaxlokk Bay. She was quickly spotted here and the next day she was hit and set on fire, rolling over and sinking in very shallow water. In the days that followed, her precious cargo of fuel was pumped out into barges through her bottom plates and shipped in triumph along to Grand Harbour.

In June, 1942 a Malta convoy from Gibraltar succeeded in getting two out of the six ships through, but of the 11 merchantmen that sailed from Alexandria at the same time, none got through. CLAN FERGUSON was back again helping to relieve Malta in August 1942, in a 14 ship convoy that included the tanker OHIO. After passing Gibraltar, the convoy had only a few hours quiet sailing before the enemy mounted a massive air attack and the carrier EAGLE was sunk. Other vessels were hit as wave after wave of bombers came over and CLAN FERGUSON escaped until just after 9 p.m. on August 12th. She was hit by a torpedo and began to settle by the stern and was also heavily ablaze with sheets of flame everywhere. Her master ordered abandon ship and 64 of her crew got clear on four rafts before being picked up by the Italians. Nine of the gallant merchantmen got through, including the badly damaged and patched-up OHIO and this convoy was the last of the great battles to Malta, for in October, the British Army blasted their way out of El Alamein to the Central Mediterranean area, thus relieving the pressure on Malta.

CLAN SKENE of 1919 was sunk by U-boat ace Peter Cremer in U333 on the 10th May, 1942, in a position 360 miles S.E. of Cape Hatteras, North Carolina while on a voyage from Cape Town to North America. Two torpedoes exploded with great force amidships blowing the bridge structure sky high. In the same month CLAN MURRAY of 1918 rescued the survivors of the P & O cargoship SOUDAN which had struck a mine off Cape Agulhas, South Africa.

In 1943 Sir August Cayzer died, his quiet restrained approach to running the company being in contrast to that of his father, and he had been an able Managing Director, as well as a Director of the Suez Canal Co. On 27th April, 1943, CLAN MACINDOE was lost after a fire and stranding at Alexandria. However, CLAN MACNAIR sailing from there on 14th September, 1943 as Commodore ship of a Malta convoy had the pleasure of seeing the main units of the Italian Navy on their way in to surrender. CLAN MACNAIR also sailed in the convoy of 36 ships from Gibraltar to Malta on 25th September and a heavy barrage was put up when the enemy aircraft flew over the convoy, but this time they stayed above the clouds. The convoy through the Mediterranean in which CLAN MACBRAYNE sailed at the end of October 1943, was attacked by submarines and 24 aircraft, of which four were shot down. The new CLAN CAMPBELL was asked to stand by the sinking U.S. transport RHONA in the Mediterranean at the end of 1943 and in the darkness rescued 149 survivors, who were taken to Phillipville, Algeria. Three days later CLAN CAMPBELL rejoined her convoy. Things had improved so much that in April, 1944 EMPIRE BARRIE, one of the standard 10,000 tons deadweight 'Empire' vessels managed by the company in the latter part of the war, and COMMANDANT DORISE, one of the French ships managed by the company and BUTESHIRE and a large convoy, sailed the full length of the Mediterranean without incident. EMPIRE BARRIE delivered more than 3,000 tons of copper to the Tyne and COMMANDANT DORISE also had 2,500 tons in a mixed cargo, while BUTESHIRE carried sisal, coffee, tea, kapok, beeswax and palm kernels.

CLAN LAMONT had been converted to a L.S.I. (Landing Ship Infantry) and took part in the North African and Italian invasions and played a leading role on D-Day. She spent most of May, 1944 carrying out pre-invasion exercises off the Isle of Wight. At the beginning of June she went into Southampton and 1400 officers and men of the Canadian Army were embarked. She sailed on the evening of 5th June and anchored in her allotted position in front of Juno beach at 6.15 a.m. on the 6th and five minutes later the first troops were heading for the shore. She made five crossings until 2nd July and carried 8,218 officers and men to Juno, Omaha and Utah beaches. She was then sent to Swansea for repairs and on 25th July she was commissioned into the Royal Navy in the Clyde as part of Force X, U.S. 7th Fleet and six days later she was renamed LAMONT. Two days later she sailed for the South West Pacific but during the Transatlantic stage she had trouble with her steering and lagged behind the convoy, continually emitting billows of black smoke. On arrival at Balboa she was rejected by the U.S. Navy. She stayed at Balboa for repairs and later continued her journey to the S.W. Pacific where she trained U.S. troops in rear areas and did some trooping. Upon the arrival of the British Pacific Fleet she was used as an accommodation ship at Manus in the Admiralty Islands, returning to Britain via the Panama Canal in early 1946.

CLAN MACARTHUR of 1912 which had been sold in 1921 to become the BERWICKSHIRE of the associated Scottish Shire Line, became the last casualty in WWII of the Clan Line and their associated fleets. She had sailed from Durban on 18th August, 1944, as Commodore ship of a small convoy bound for Tamatave and Mauritius. Three of the convoy including BERWICKSHIRE and the escort, then formed a separate slow convoy and in the early evening of 20th August, the tanker DARONIA was torpedoed. Four hours later, just when they thought they had lost the submarine, BERWICKSHIRE was torpedoed amidships and the survivors abandoned ship before a second torpedo smashed in. The old ship died slowly and 94 survivors were picked up the following morning, but 8 had died in the blast.

The ADOLPH S. OCHS, one of 12 standard 'Liberty' ships managed during the war by the company, had been on Russian convoys before, when she left in a big convoy for Russia at the beginning of February 1945. The convoy was twice attacked by large formations of torpedo-bombers which were mostly dealt with by carrier based fighters and at least eight were shot down. One blade of the propeller of ADOLPH S.

OCHS was badly bent whilst following an icebreaker into Molotovsk and, after partial discharge, she was towed to Archangel to complete discharge. However she was able to sail back at reduced speed arriving safely on 31st March. After exchanging propellers she sailed to New York, where her torpedo-net booms were removed, then voyaged to the warmer climes of Gibraltar and Bari and on to sun-baked South American ports.

7. POST WORLD WAR II.

Clan Line then set about rebuilding the fleet after the heavy losses and the gap was plugged initially by nine 'Empires', nine 'Oceans' and two 'Liberties'. A large building programme of steam and diesel cargo-liners was embarked upon in 1946 starting with the six vessels of the 'MACL.' class. They were of 8,800 tons deadweight with the dimensions length 445 feet, breadth 61 feet and draft 26 feet. Two of the class, CLAN MACLENNAN and CLAN MACLACHLAN, had steam turbines while the rest had diesels. They were distinguished by three pairs of kingposts, each with one heavy and four smaller derricks. Two single posts stood immediately in front of the bridge and behind the superstructure. Topmasts were carried on the first pair of kingposts and on the pair aft of the superstructure. The diesel-engined CLAN MACLAREN, CLAN MACLEAN, CLAN MACLEOD and CLAN MACLAY were to give considerably longer service to Clan Line than the two steamers of the class, which were all completed at Greenock Dockyard.

In 1948 Clan Line re-entered the passenger trade, with 14 of their ships offering accommodation for 12 first class passengers and filled a much needed demand. Two turbine-driven sisters of 8035 gross tons, CLAN MACTAVISH and CLAN MACTAGGART, were then completed in 1949 by Greenock Dockyard. Heavy derricks of 125 tons capacity, the heaviest ever fitted to a Clan Line vessel at that time, were carried on all three masts with a top mast on the second and on the one aft. A lattice navigation mast of pyramid shape stood on the monkey island above the bridge. They had pole main and mizzen masts rather than kingposts. At this time the white upper parts of the hull including the bulwarks were being extended three feet down the hull, and CLAN MACTAVISH and CLAN MACTAGGART were the first new ships to have this feature and gave them and all subsequent ships, especially the 'S' class, an enhanced appearance. CLAN MACTAVISH sailed from Middlesbrough in April, 1962 for Australia with two complete Linz & Donowitz steel furnaces weighing 1300 tons for the Broken Hill Proprietary Co. Ltd., of Newcastle N.S.W. Both vessels were sold for scrap in 1971.

CLAN SHAW, first of the 'S' class and the beginning of the second phase of war replacements, was then launched on 23rd August, 1949, by Lady Rotherwick at Greenock for their South, East and Round Africa services. She had five holds, was of mixed welded/riveted construction, 8101 gross tons with a deadweight of 11,000 tons carried on two continuous decks below the weather deck and split by eight transverse bulkheads to give fifteen cargo spaces. She had a cruiser spoon stern and a broad funnel with a very distinctive cowl on top. The funnel was known as the 'Helmet' and ensured efficient smoke dispersal away from passenger accommodation and disguised the extra height of the smoke stack whilst showing off the company colours to the best advantage. She was well finished inside with accommodation for twelve passengers, heightening the superstructure by one deck, which in most respects was superior to that of passenger liners of the time, consisting of two double and eight single staterooms with bathroom and toilet en-suite. Length overall was 512 feet, breadth was 66 feet and draft was 27 feet, with cargo-gear in abundance consisting of a 60-ton heavy lift and a 30-tonner on the second mast, with a 30-tonner on the mast aft, two 15-ton, two 7-ton and twelve 5-ton derricks and electric cargo winches. The weather deck covers were a mixture of hatch board and beam. Later ships had slab covers, particularly if the vessel was trading to Australia where this was compulsory. There was also wooden panelling on the front of the monkey island above the bridge. Babcock and Wilcox boilers and the well tried Wallsend-Howden oil-burners and Parsons geared turbines gave 10,000 shp and propelled her at 17 knots.

CLAN SHAW made her maiden voyage to South Africa on 25th January, 1950, under the command of Capt. R. P. Galer C.B.E. In 1953 she represented the company at the Coronation Review and was commanded for the occasion by Capt. H. J. Anchor O.B.E., who was invited for presentation to the Queen on board H.M.S.

SURPRISE. The number four 'tween deck was converted into a carpeted overflow lounge to cope with the large number of company guests aboard. In 1955 talks began with the board of Union-Castle Line and in 1956 Clan Line Steamers Ltd. merged with Union-Castle Line to form the British and Commonwealth Shipping Company, a £53M amalgamation. Lord Rotherwick had achieved the merger after many years of competition on the South African route and served as the first B. & C. Chairman until his death in 1958, when he was succeeded by his nephew Sir Nicholas Cayzer, elder son of Sir August Cayzer. Among the Union-Castle subsidiaries taken over was the long-established Bullard, King Line whose ships, with names beginning UM-, sailing rights and equity were transferred to a newly-established South African company, the Springbok Line in 1959. This was a paper transaction involving the exchange of shares and was a precautionary measure taken in case flag discrimination was practised against British ships. CLAN SHAW was transferred to this company in 1960 becoming STEENBOK. The following year a full merger took place between Springbok Line and Safmarine and she was renamed SOUTH AFRICAN SEAFARER. Shortly after being renamed S.A. SEAFARER in 1966, she ran aground in darkness and heavy seas on 1st July, 1966 off the Green Point Light just outside Cape Town harbour while inward bound from Glasgow with 63 crew and 12 passengers aboard including a six-month old baby. All were rescued at daybreak by helicopter, the ship having earlier broken her back. For weeks after the stranding the cargo, consisting of 7,800 tons of chemicals and thousands of bottles of whisky, drifted ashore and several months later the weather had made the wreck almost unrecognisable and was eventually broken up by a local scrap metal company. The master had his certificate suspended for two years at the subsequent inquiry.

CLAN SINCLAIR was launched next at Greenock on 17th January, 1950 and made her maiden voyage in April, 1950. She was a regular caller at Mauritius to load bagged sugar at anchor from barges. She followed the same pattern of renamings as her sister, becoming BOSBOK in 1960, SOUTH AFRICAN STATESMAN in 1961, S.A.

STATESMAN in 1966 and arrived at Kaohsiung on 3rd November, 1972 to be broken up.

CLAN SUTHERLAND was launched on 28th December, 1950, the ceremony being performed by the Duchess of Sutherland. Successful trials were held in the Clyde on 30th March, 1951 and the ship left Birkenhead on 28th April, 1951 for South Africa on her maiden voyage under the command of Capt. H. J. Anchor O.B.E. She discharged and loaded at Beira and came home via Suez. In December, 1960 her original 65-ton derrick was replaced by the largest heavy-lift gear in the Clan Line fleet, a 180-tonner with a SWL of 165 tons on the short mast between Nos. 1 and 2 holds and was the principal reason why she was retained by the company long after her sisters were sold. The mast was heavily stayed by steel rods connecting the top of the mast to strongpoints on the deck, and at least six Clarke Chapman winches were used to operate the massive derrick. The derrick was fitted by Greenock Dockyard, and was designed to work with maximum load at 12 ft 6 ins outreach, which was increased to about 20 feet with a heel of 10°. It was tested with a load of 181.5 tons with the vessel ballasted with oil fuel and water, and the angle of heel was 8.5°. The total weight of the new equipment fitted was 205 tons but CLAN SUTHERLAND was still able to take deck loads on No. 2 hatch as the deck was clear of obstruction. Some examples of heavy single lifts made using this gear were a 162-ton stator taken from Birkenhead to South Africa in 1964, a 100-ton plus paper mill cylinder for Transvaal in 1966 and a 148-ton transformer taken from Genoa to Port Elizabeth in January, 1969. She also ran to Australia many times in her career with her first visit in November, 1952, making good profits on large items of machinery for steel mills in Newcastle, N.S.W. These freight charges alone usually paid for the whole voyage, so any cargo homeward from Australia was profit all the way. On one trip she loaded a 152-ton stator for Sydney, a 162-ton stator for Melbourne and a 91-ton turbo-alternator for Fremantle. She was involved in a nasty fire at Beira in 1954, when an oil leak from an up-river berth ignited between herself and the wharf. The ship was working cargo at the time and there was some loss of life among native cargo workers and also the ship's doctor who suffocated down a hold when thick smoke engulfed them. Her captain, Capt. A. G. Storkey was awarded the O.B.E. in the 1955 Birthday Honours for his actions on that occasion. The fire had occurred only a week after CLAN SUTHERLAND had been in collision with the Italian ship RINANO as she entered Beira. CLAN SUTHERLAND served the Clan Line well until 10th November, 1971 the day she was delivered to Chinese mainland breakers at Hsingkiang.

CLAN SHAW, CLAN SINCLAIR and CLAN SUTHERLAND were part of a five ship order, Yard Nos. 471-5 from Greenock Dockyard, but before building commenced 473 and 474, to be named CLAN SKENE and CLAN STEWART respectively, were sold to the Pacific Steam Navigation Company becoming their KENUTA and FLAMENCO. The Pacific Steam Navigation Company subsequently built three more identical sisters to 'S' class, COTOPAXI from W. Denny, POTOSI and PIZARRO from Greenock Dockyard, the only minor difference being the installation of mechanical hold ventilation.

In 1950 Clan Line were operating a fleet of 48 steamers and motorships, none of which was more than 20 years old. In 1951-52 three smaller motor vessels of 9,000 tons deadweight were built, CLAN MACINNES, CLAN MACINTOSH and CLAN MACINTYRE, the last two by John Brown at Clydebank. They had two low crosstree masts to serve the forward holds and one aft, each with four derricks. A heavy derrick was fitted on the second mast and on the one aft, while two more pairs of derricks stood on posts immediately in front of the bridge and behind the superstructure. Again the motor vessels lasted longer in service than the steamers, CLAN MACINTOSH being scrapped as SANIL in 1980 and CLAN MACINNES late in 1979 as ATHOUB. CLAN MACINTYRE came to grief when as EASTERN EXPRESS, she was aground south of La Spezia at Marina di Carrara as she left port for Sardinia, and was declared a total loss. A gale had driven her ashore on 22nd December, 1979 and she ended up on the beach with a heavy list to starboard.

The Thompson Steam Shipping Co. Ltd. was acquired in 1952, together with three standard WWII types; AMERSHAM ex EMPIRE ENVOY, CHELTENHAM ex

EMPIRE RAIN and FARNINGHAM ex OCEAN VESTAL. FARNINGHAM was transferred to the British and South American Steam Navigation Co. Ltd., being renamed HELLENES and subsequently in 1957 registered under Clan Line Steamers Ltd. and the other two were sold. The management of three tankers of the Scottish Tanker Company, a Cayzer, Irvine subsidiary, was transferred to the Thompson management company of Huntley, Cook Ltd.

An unusual exercise was carried out in 1953 when two pontoon barges were chopped in half at Swansea, reducing each heavy lift to 65 tons and enabling them to be lifted aboard and discharged using the vessel's own gear at their destination of Aden, where they were to be the base of a 100-ton floating crane. The first half-barge with dimensions 50 feet by 40 feet by 6 feet 6 inches depth, was loaded aboard CLAN CAMPBELL of 1944 with her own 80-ton derrick. The usual method of lifting using wire legs could not be used because of the headroom restriction on the ship and so details of the barge were sent to the naval architect at Greenock Dockyard, who calculated from them the centre of gravity of the barge and designed a short lifting beam with steadying legs and connecting shackle and ancillary gear. The beam was fabricated at Greenock Dockyard and dispatched to the barge at Swansea where it was bolted to its predetermined position on its deck. The centre of gravity of the barge section was immediately beneath the beam's lifting points, and the deck was specially strengthened to receive the beam. The barge section was put aboard without hitch on 11th May and lowered onto prepared timber beds on No. 2 hatch and its adjacent deck with the bulk of the barge slightly off centre towards the port side, so as to leave a clear walking and working way on the starboard side. The other half-barge was lifted aboard CLAN LAMONT on 3rd June, and the two halves of the second barge were transported to Aden by CLAN MACTAVISH, one on top of the other on No. 2 hatch.

CLAN STEWART was launched on 22nd October, 1953 by Hon. Mrs. Robin Cayzer, trials were run on 22nd January, 1954 and she sailed on her maiden voyage to South Africa on 17th March, 1954 again under the command of Capt. H. J. Anchor

O.B.E. In 1961 she was transferred to Safmarine and renamed SOUTH AFRICAN SCULPTOR. However, she was transferred back the following year and renamed KINPURNIE CASTLE, sailing with Clan Line officers and a Zulu crew. She and CLAN SUTHERLAND acted as the British and Commonwealth Group Cadet ships at this time with a dozen cadets being given their first trip at sea in them each voyage, a sickening thought! CLAN SUTHERLAND made her first cadet voyage to Australia leaving the U.K. at the end of September, 1964. In 1967 KINPURNIE CASTLE just managed to get out of Port Said and Alexandria before the Suez Canal was closed by the Arab-Israeli war, and later that year was sold to Astro Firme S.A., Panama and renamed HELLENIC MED. She arrived at Gadani Beach on 15th March, 1978 for scrapping.

Clan Line then had CLAN ROBERTSON and CLAN ROSS built at Greenock with longer 174-feet bridge superstructures but similar dimensions and cargo capacity to the 'S' class. They were considered by many people to be the most handsome ships in the post-war Clan Line fleet. They had 105-ton derrick and a full complement of 40, 15, 7 and 5-ton derricks with a pair of posts instead of a single mast at No. 4 hold as in the 'S' class. CLAN ROBERTSON was launched on 17th March, 1954 by Hon. Mrs. Anthony Cayzer and sailed for South Africa in June of that year on her maiden voyage. She loaded many export cargoes at Birkenhead for South Africa and was transferred to Bullard, King in 1959 and renamed UMZINTO. In 1960 she was transferred to the Springbok Line and renamed ROOIBOK and in 1961 to Safmarine and renamed SOUTH AFRICAN SHIPPER becoming S.A. SHIPPER in 1966. On 26th November, 1975 she arrived at Kaohsiung for scrapping.

CLAN ROSS was launched on 17th January, 1955 by Miss Nichola Cayzer. CLAN ROSS was transferred to Safmarine in 1961 and renamed SOUTH AFRICAN SCIENTIST. However, she was transferred back in 1962 and renamed KINNAIRD CASTLE and sailed with Clan Line officers and a Zulu crew. She made a round voyage to Australia in late 1967 through to the Spring of 1968. She departed from Rotterdam on 21st November, 1967, called at Antwerp, Las Palmas and Durban, then went on to Fremantle, Albany, Port Pirie, Adelaide, Melbourne and Sydney to load wool throughout January, 1968, and returned via Cape Town to discharge at Dunkirk, Flushing and Liverpool, where she arrived on 1st April, 1968. She then went round to South Shields for dry-docking and special survey and departed on 30th April. She was also a Cadet ship, normally carrying 4 or 6 cadets, half being engineer cadets, half deck cadets. She had a record wait of four months and ten days at anchor at Lobito, Angola from October, 1974 to February, 1975 before berthing to discharge. Later in 1975 she was sold to Dasonab Nav. S.A. and renamed NAZEER and was often seen in Aqaba and her old Red Sea haunts until she arrived at Gadani Beach on 26th April, 1978 for scrapping.

ARGYLLSHIRE and AYRSHIRE were similar in appearance but took Scottish Shire Line names. They were part refrigerated for the Australian meat, wool, fruit and dairy produce trades. Deadweight was 11,240 tons and total cargo capacity was 629,350 cu. ft. of which 378,000 cu. ft. was refrigerated. They had six holds with three complete decks in Nos. 1, 2, 3 and 4 holds and two decks in Nos. 5 and 6 holds, with refrigeration in Nos. 2, 3, 4 holds and lower tweendecks, and No. 5 hold and upper tweendeck. Special consideration was given to the quick handling of refrigerated cargo and also for the stowage of wool in bales. There were twelve 5-ton, four 7-ton and four 15-ton derricks and for heavy lifts, a 105-tonner on the mainmast with 40-tonners on the main and aft masts. There was excellent accommodation for the 28 officers, 73 crew and 12 passengers. Length overall was 535 feet, breadth was 69 feet and draft was 28 feet. The Parsons reaction turbines gave 10,500 shp and 17 knots at service speed, and flat-out gave 11,500 shp and 19 knots.

ARGYLLSHIRE was launched on 23rd May, 1956, at Greenock Dockyard by Countess Jellicoe and sailed on her maiden voyage to Durban on 15th November, 1956 under Capt. A. J. Hogg, carrying a 103-ton stator for delivery at Melbourne. In 1964 she loaded an exceptionally long 98-ton boiler for Port Elizabeth at Birkenhead. She subsequently became the Group flag ship until she was sold for further service to Gulf East Marine in 1975 and renamed SCHIVAGO, and then on 3rd August, 1977 arrived at Gadani Beach for scrapping. AYRSHIRE was launched on 19th October, 1956 by the Countess of Powis and left on her maiden voyage to Australia on 25th May, 1957 under the command of Clan Line Commodore Capt. P. Macmillan. On 23rd March, 1965 she ran aground on the island of Abd Al Kuri, 430 miles E.S.E. of Aden near the island of Socotra. There was no loss of life and some 1350 tons of cargo was off-loaded and landed at Aden by barge. On 26th April, 1965 she was refloated briefly, but ran aground again and salvage was abandoned on 28th April. A sad end to such a fine ship was compounded by the fact that Capt. Macmillan was on his retirement voyage.

An account of a Clan Line voyage to East Africa and Australia made at this time may be instructive. CLAN CAMPBELL, a steamer built in 1944, left King George V Dock, Glasgow on 22nd June, 1955 under the command of Capt. H.C. Simpson for Birkenhead to complete loading. They sailed on 30th June on the Clan-Hall-Harrison service to East Africa and passed Cape St. Vincent with its famous cliff-top lighthouse on 4th July and entered the Strait of Gibraltar later that day. They stopped at Algiers for fuel and water on 6th July and threaded their way in through the narrow channel into Port Said on 11th July. After transiting the Canal via the Bitter Lakes they went straight down the Red Sea missing the brown menace of the blinding sandstorms as well as Port Sudan, Massawa and Djibouti and arrived at Aden for more bunkers on 17th July. They left the same day and reached Mombasa on 23rd July to discharge. Tanga with its beautiful cove was next stop on 3rd August, then on to Dar-Es-Salaam, reached on 10th August for final discharge. Here, as at Mombasa, football matches were played with neighbouring freighters, but instead of returning home as planned on the Clan-Hall-Harrison service, they were suddenly ordered to sail in ballast to pick up a grain and wool cargo in Australia. They left Dar on 13th August and rolled for 16 days to Fremantle, reached on 29th August for bunkers. They arrived at Port Pirie on a beautiful sunny Sunday morning, 4th September, in company with CLAN MACINNES. The short haul round to Adelaide was made the following week and arrived 11th September to complete loading of grain and wool. They returned to

Fremantle on the return leg on 26th September where CLAN SINCLAIR was lying on the other side of the harbour and they left the beautiful Swan River on 28th September and rolled for 9 days to Cochin where they changed Indian crews, calling at Colombo on the way for water. They took more bunkers at Aden on the 15th October before entering Suez on the 20th to take the north-bound convoy which anchored as usual in the Bitter Lakes to let the south-bound convoy through. They passed Pantelleria with its well-terraced vineyards and large fishing port at the western end on the 24th, followed by Gibraltar, Ushant and docked at Dunkirk to discharge on 1st November. After more discharging at Hull, they arrived back at Liverpool on 11th November and signed off the following day. The round voyage to East Africa and Australia took 4 months and 12 days and was only slightly longer than the normal duration of an Indian voyage which averaged 3-4 months. This would typically call to load tea at either Calcutta or Chittagong on the east coast, or Cochin or Tuticorin on the west coast, the last named actually lying on the southern-most tip of India. Coming south from Calcutta the ports used would be Vizagapatnam to load ore and tobacco at the winding river berths, Coconada for palmyra fibre and tobacco, Madras for ore, tobacco, leather, crushed bones, magnesite and cotton material and finally Pondicherry to load cotton material goods. Onto Ceylon (or Sri Lanka as it is now called) with the ports of Trincomalee and Galle being much used in preference to the harbour congestion at Colombo, loading tea and rubber. The vessels on the South African service might call at Las Palmas for bunkers, where officers would change from blue uniforms to tropical 'whites', Walvis Bay, Cape Town, Port Elizabeth, East London, Durban and return to the U.K. taking 3-4 months for the round voyage, or head for East African ports via Lourenco Marques, Beira, Mtwara, Tanga, Dar-Es-Salaam, Mombasa and then home, or perhaps a 'double-header' voyage to the Mediterranean to discharge and then reload for South Africa, and then onto the U.K. taking around 10 months all told.

Internal fighting in Sri Lanka is nothing new, and CLAN MACKINNON, built 1945, was commandeered for a mercy mission in Colombo in June, 1958 after the first flare-up of fighting between Tamils and Cinghalese. She was requisitioned by the Royal Ceylon Navy after discharging 5,500 tons of general cargo, and loaded 600 Tamils for transport to Kankessantuari in the north of the island and took two days to reach there via the southern coast. At daylight on the third day, landfall was made at Point Pedro and after discharging the Tamils, loaded 67 Cinghalese for the trip back to Colombo, where CLAN MACKINNON was returned to her owners.

The record for the highest number of company vessels in port together at Beira was nine, this occurring in July, 1950 with four alongside at the harbour berths, four at the buoys or at anchor in the river and one at the Bar. The vessels concerned were CLANs CUMMING, CHISHOLM, FORBES, ALLAN, MACBRAYNE, MACLEAN, MACBRIDE, MACBETH and the BUTESHIRE. This topped the next previous best of seven vessels in July, 1963 these being CLANs MACLAREN, MACTAGGART, MACIVER, FINLAY and ARGYLLSHIRE, STIRLINGSHIRE and KENILWORTH CASTLE. Five were loading for the U.K. with the remaining two discharging cargo, which for ARGYLLSHIRE also consisted of a 100-ton transformer. The disposition of the 49 Clan vessels in the company fleet on 1st September, 1956 showed surprisingly only one vessel, CLAN MACLENNAN, in port at Beira, with only three others CLAN MACLEOD, CLAN MACDOUGALL, CLAN MACTAGGART voyaging to or from Australia.

The 'S' class and their derivatives were the last steamers of the Clan Line, and the switch to diesels for all subsequent vessels started with the three 'M' class CLAN MALCOLM, CLAN MATHESON and CLAN MENZIES which appeared in 1957-58. Their looks were similar to the 'S' class, although without the large funnel cowl and their deadweight was 1,000 tons less than the 'S' class for the route out to India. CLAN MALCOLM was a Cadet ship in the late sixties. They gave good service until the late seventies when CLAN MATHESON arrived at Kaohsiung breakers on 12th December, 1978 with the other two being sold off the following year.

Clan Line then started building a class of sixteen 'Three-quarters aft' motor vessels, with the first fifteen built between 1958-63. They had five holds, four forward of the superstructure and one aft. CLAN MACIVER was the lead ship, built by Greenock Dockyard, although she and CLAN MACILWRAITH of 1960 were smaller than the rest with a deadweight of 10,000 tons. These two, and the larger CLAN MACINDOE of 1959 had three low bipod masts with two heavy lift derricks on the third mast, aft were four derricks on two pairs of posts giving a total of 16 derricks. The superstructure was continued aft to merge with the poop structure. Then in 1961-62 came CLAN FORBES, CLAN FERGUSSON, CLAN FRASER, CLAN FARQUHARSON, CLAN FINLAY, CLAN GRAHAM, CLAN GRANT, CLAN MACNAB and CLAN MACNAIR of 12,000 tons deadweight and dimensions; length 508 feet, breadth 63 feet and draft 28 feet. These differed from the earlier three by having ordinary crosstree masts forward and only two derricks on one set of posts aft. Then in 1962-63 came CLAN MACGILLIVRAY, CLAN MACGREGOR and CLAN MACGOWAN of similar size, but the superstructure was not continued along to the poop, and a single crosstree mast was placed right aft, replacing the pair of posts. These were more highly automated with the engine room designed so that one engineer officer and an assistant could maintain watch.

Nine of the sixteen were built at Greenock Dockyard if one includes CLAN ALPINE, the final vessel completed in 1967. Greenock Dockyard itself a British and Commonwealth Group subsidiary, had by that time been taken over by the adjoining Scotts' yard on 1st April, 1966. CLAN ALPINE was the 67th Clan or British and Commonwealth cargo-liner built at the yard; and altogether was the 133rd Clan vessel to have come from Clyde yards, including those from the Ayrshire Dockyard at Irvine - a glowing tribute indeed to the local yards. CLAN ALPINE was similar to the CLAN MACGREGOR trio, but had only one lifeboat on each side instead of the usual two, and had a larger winch-house on the second mast. Two of the class, CLAN MACINDOE and CLAN MACNAIR, were built by John Brown at Clydebank, while the remaining five 'F' vessels were built at the Tyneside yard of Swan, Hunter & Wigham Richardson Ltd. These five were to provide a monthly service between Liverpool and the Persian Gulf, however, Clan Line surprised everyone by selling two of these to India in 1965, and the remaining three to Iran in 1968. CLAN FORBES and CLAN

FINLAY were to meet up again on at least one occasion, as in November 1971 they were loading at Birkenhead as ARYA MAN for Callao, Peru and as ATLANTIC OCEAN for China respectively. CLAN MACGOWAN was sold in 1969 to India becoming INDIAN TRIBUNE, and as such was severely damaged by collision whilst berthed at Bombay on 16th April, 1979 but however was repaired. Unusual heavy lifts in the sixties were three giant petroleum reactors taken from Italy by CLAN MACGREGOR to the Caltex refinery at Milnerton, Cape Town in April, 1965; four Australian yachts loaded at Sydney by CLAN MACGOWAN in 1968 and discharged at Dunkirk in time for Cowes Week; heavy 104-ton transformers and stators taken by CLAN MACTAVISH from Birkenhead, where she loaded them with her own gear, to Port Elizabeth in 1963; and a 66 feet long trawler stowed athwart the No. 3 hatch of CLAN FERGUSSON and taken to Chittagong in December, 1962. CLAN MACLEAN must surely take the prize for unusual items however, for she loaded two 'Lightning' fighters for Aden at Belfast in May 1961!

5. CLAN LAMONT completed 1879 by Alexander Stephen was one of the original set of 6 steamers. From a painting.

6. CLAN BUCHANAN of 1882 photographed in Table Bay.
(A. Duncan).

7. CLAN MATHESON of 1883 photographed in the Suez Canal.
(W.S.P.L.).

8. CLAN MACARTHUR of 1882 was a sister of CLAN MATHESON and one of a class of 4 steel steamers, the first built for the company. *(W.S.P.L.).*

9. CLAN CAMPBELL of 1894 was one of a class of 6 steamers built at Barrow. *(A. Duncan).*

10. CLAN CHISHOLM of 1896 was built by Alexander Stephen, and was sold to Japan and wrecked there in 1926. *(York Collection).*

11. CLAN COLQUHOUN was a Turret built in 1899, and was sold to Italy and broken up there in 1929. *J.K. Byass).*

12. CLAN URQUHART was a Turret built in 1899, and was sold to Germany and broken up in Stettin in 1933. *(York Collection).*

13. CLAN FERGUSON was a Turret built in 1898 and was one of two built at Barrow under licence from William Doxford. *(A. Duncan).*

14. CLAN LINDSAY was a Turret built in 1902 and was broken up in Inverkeithing in 1931. *(W.S.P.L.).*

15. CLAN CHATTAN was a Turret built in 1902 and was broken up at Bo'ness in 1930. *(A. Duncan).*

16. CLAN BUCHANAN was the last Turret built in 1907 and was broken up at Blyth in 1933. *(B. Feilden).*

17. CLAN MACGILLIVRAY completed on the Tyne in 1911 had the longest career for the company of any CLAN. *(Builders photo).*

18. CLAN OGILVY of 1914 was the first company vessel with a cruiser stern and was built by William Doxford. *(York Collection).*

19. CLAN ROSS of 1914 at Cape Town was a sister of CLAN OGILVY and one of three sisters from different builders, this one built on the Tyne by Swan, Hunter & Wigham Richardson Ltd. *(Solomon).*

20. CLAN STUART of 1916 was sunk by collision in the English Channel in March, 1940. *(J. Clarkson).*

21. CLAN KENNETH was built as ARDGRYFE in 1909 and purchased by the company in 1918. *(York Collection).*

22. CLAN MACINNES was completed by Lithgows in 1920 and broken up at Calcutta in 1955. *(B. Feilden).*

23. CLAN MURDOCH was completed by Ayrshire Dockyard in 1919 and sank off Lisbon in 1953. *(J. Clarkson).*

24. CLAN MURRAY of 1918 photographed in Table Bay was broken up at Bo'ness in 1952. *(W.S.P.L.).*

25. CLAN MACNAIR was completed by Ayrshire Dockyard and broken up at Blyth in 1952. *(B. Feilden).*

26. CLAN MACDOUGALL of 1929 and CLAN MACDONALD were the first company vessels with diesel engines. *(B. Feilden).*

27. CLAN MACPHERSON of 1929 reverted to triple expansion steam engines. *(J. Clarkson)*.

28. CLAN GRANT was completed in 1912 by Hawthorn, Leslie as PORT MACQUARIE and purchased in 1929. *(A. Duncan).*

29. CLAN COLQUHOUN built in 1918 was formerly the White Star Line GALLIC before being purchased in 1933. *(B. Feilden).*

30. CLAN URQUHART was completed in 1911 as ARGYLLSHIRE for Scottish Shire Line and transferred to Clan Line in 1933. *(J. Clarkson)*.

31. CLAN MACAULAY and CLAN MACARTHUR of 1936 were the start of a big building programme. *(F.R. Sherlock)*.

32. CLAN CHATTAN of 1937 was a Malta convoy heroine. *(A. Duncan).*

33. CLAN CAMPBELL of 1937 was another Malta convoy heroine. *(A. Duncan).*

34. CLAN CAMERON of 1937 survived the war and was broken up at Hong Kong in 1959. *(F.R. Sherlock).*

35. CLAN MACRAE of 1942 was one of the CLAN CAMERON class but was completed as EMPIRE MIGHT. *(L. Baker).*

36. CLAN DAVIDSON of 1943 had a magnificent war record as a midget submarine depot ship. *(W.T. Hubbard).*

37. CLAN ALPINE built in 1942 as EMPIRE BARRIE at Sunderland and purchased in 1945 ended up in a paddy field near Chittagong in 1960 and was scrapped 'as lies'. *(B. Feilden).*

38. CLAN MACFADYEN was a 'Liberty' vessel completed in 1944 as SAMDERWENT and purchased in 1947. *(J. Clarkson).*

39. CLAN MACQUEEN was completed in 1942 as OCEAN VESPER and is photographed at Mombasa. *(Clansman).*

40. CLAN CHISHOLM built 1944 photographed entering Dublin.
(P. Sweeney).

41. CLAN CAMPBELL built 1943 photographed in the English Channel. *(Skyfotos Ltd.)*.

42. CLAN MACLENNAN completed in 1947 was one of 6 sisters.
(B. Feilden).

43. CLAN MACLEAN of 1947 photographed at Vizaghapatnam.
(Clansman).

44. CLAN SHAW of 1950, first of the 'S' class photographed in the Mersey. *(Mersey Photos)*.

45. CLAN SINCLAIR of 1950 loading sugar from barges at Mauritius. *(Clansman).*

46. CLAN SUTHERLAND of 1951 seen on trials. *(W. Ralston Ltd.).*

47. CLAN SUTHERLAND lifting a 162-ton stator at Gladstone Dock, Liverpool. *(Stewart Bale Ltd.)*.

48. CLAN STEWART of 1954 seen leaving the Tyne. *(G.R. Scott).*

49. CLAN ROBERTSON of 1954 at speed. *(Builders photograph).*

50. CLAN ROBERTSON of 1954 in the Mersey. *(B. Fielden).*

51. CLAN ROSS of 1956 seen on trials. *(Clansman).*

52. ARGYLLSHIRE of 1956 seen on trials. *(Clansman).*

53. The ill-fated AYRSHIRE of 1957. *(W. Ralston Ltd.)*.

54. CLAN MATHESON of 1957 seen on trials. *(Clansman).*

55. CLAN MENZIES of 1958 seen leaving the Tyne in 1979 following pre-sale dry-docking inspection. *(G.R. Scott).*

56. CLAN MACINDOE of 1959 photographed in the English Channel. *(Skyfotos Ltd.).*

57. CLAN MACIVER of 1958 at Cape Town. *(Clansman).*

58. CLAN MACNAIR of 1962 at Cape Town. *(J.K. de Vries Jnr.).*

59. CLAN FRASER seen afloat in the Tyne after launching on 27th July 1961. *(Clansman).*

60. CLAN FINLAY seen afloat in the Tyne after launching on 29th June 1962. *(Clansman).*

61. CLAN FORBES fitting-out on the Tyne in May 1961. *(G.R. Scott).*

62. CLAN MACGILLIVRAY seen shortly before launch at Greenock Dockyard in May 1962 with a good general view of the yard. *(Clansman).*

63. CLAN RANALD being launched at Greenock Dockyard on 21st December 1964. *(Clansman)*.

64. CLAN ALPINE, the last CLAN, being launched at Greenock Dockyard on 1st December 1966. *(Clansman).*

65. CLAN ALPINE photographed in the English Channel. *(Skyfotos Ltd.).*

66. CLAN ROSS of 1966 photographed in the English Channel.
(Skyfotos Ltd.).

67. ARGYLLSHIRE passing Calshot Radar Station in Southampton Water in 1973. *(A. Greenway).*

68. Vittoria Dock, Birkenhead, as it is today with the last visible evidence of the CLAN LINE near the roof of the warehouse. *(Author).*

8. FINAL RUN-DOWN.

This was very rapid, especially so in the years 1979 to 1981. The container revolution had already started when CLAN ALPINE was fitting out in early 1967 and management gave a clear indication of their intentions by selecting this name for their last ship, for it was also the first ship in 1878. The last CLAN ALPINE sailed from Middlesbrough on her maiden voyage to South and East Africa on 21st April, 1967 under the command of Capt. N. F. Stewart. The fleet at that time consisted of 41 vessels and the run-down of ships on the India route started in the early seventies with the early post-war steamers and motor vessels, gathering momentum in the middle seventies with more departures from the fleet, with only 24 vessels left in 1973 and 13 vessels left in 1978 and reached a climax when only the remaining ten vessels of the 'Three-quarters aft' class were left in 1979, and these were disposed of during the next two years. The last ten were divided equally between the Indian and East African trades, with the port of Nicala, Mozambique figuring prominently in the latter's destination lists. CLAN MACGREGOR made the final Clan Line voyage by arriving back at Avonmouth on 1st November, 1981. She moved round to the Mersey and departed from there under new owners, but was to last only tens months more in service, for on 9th November, 1982 she became a total loss due to fire damage, when 60 miles south of Cyprus. She was towed to Larnaca and subsequently to Laurium for scrapping. CLAN MACGILLIVRAY had made the last east bound voyage and arrived at Calcutta at about the same time as CLAN MACGREGOR had arrived at Avonmouth, and she was immediately sold to Hong Kong buyers who gave her a new Clan name, CLAN MACBOYD, which had never been used in the company fleet.

The story is not quite complete however, for in 1965-66 Clan Line had four reefers built as the last order from Greenock Dockyard. CLAN RAMSAY, CLAN RANALD, CLAN ROBERTSON and CLAN ROSS, the last named being the last ship built at the Dockyard, were built for the seasonal fruit trade from South Africa and off season were usually laid up at Southampton. CLAN RANALD made Clan Line history in October, 1967 when she was the first vessel to sail into Durban flying the blue Royal Mail pennant. CLAN ROSS also flew the pennant when she sailed on the same day on the homeward leg; both were deputising for GOOD HOPE CASTLE while away on refit. In comparison to the early vessels they were devoid of sheer. They kept their Clan names until 1976-77 when they took Union-Castle colours becoming WINCHESTER CASTLE, DOVER CASTLE, BALMORAL CASTLE and KINPURNIE CASTLE respectively. The word CASTLE was dropped in preference to UNIVERSAL in 1979 and they were sold out to Greek owners in 1981-82 and ended their days at the breakers in 1984-85.

Today the cranes, slipways, hammer-head and fitting-out quay of Greenock Dockyard are still in existence, although quietly deteriorating away, and the British and Commonwealth Group have moved out of shipping and, backed by the vast assets of the Cayzer fortune, have diversified with interests in helicopters, engineering, hotels, canning, timber, investment trusts, banking, insurance and computerised information services. There are now no Clan Line vessels reported as trading, although the exact fate of CLAN MENZIES of 1958 and CLAN FINLAY of 1962 as the Chinese XING LONG and LU CHUN respectively, is not known.

FLEET LIST NOTES

Vessels are listed in order of date of launch, or in the case of second-hand tonnage, date of purchase and details are to World Ship Society standard format.

The notation (1), (2) etc. after a ship's name indicates that she is the first, the second etc.. ship of that name in the fleet. The dates following the name are those of entering and leaving the fleet, or coming under and leaving the management of the company.

On the first line is given the ship's Official Number (O.N.) in the British Registry, followed by her tonnages ('g') and net ('n'). Dimensions given are registered length x beam x depth in feet and tenths. On the second line is given the type and make of engine and name of the engine builders. T.3-cyl. denotes triple expansion three cylinder steam engines, Q.4-cyl. denotes quadruple expansion four cylinder steam engines, and for motor vessels the number of cylinders is given and whether they are two stroke cycle (2SC) or four stroke cycle (4SC), single acting (SA) or double acting (DA). Nhp denotes nominal horse power, shp shaft horse power, bhp brake horse power, and ihp indicated horse power.

APPENDIX 1
VESSELS OWNED

S1. JALAWAR (1876–1878)
O.N. 11996. 655 g. 635 n. 138.8x32.4x22.0 ft. Sailing ship.
1850 launched at Liverpool as JALAWAR for Moore and Co., Liverpool. *1871* sold to T. Holderness, Liverpool. *1876* Purchased by C.W. Cayzer. *1878* transferred to Cayzer, Irvine and Co. *17.11.1878* foundered off Java Head.

S2. NORTH STAR (1877–1880)
O.N. 52866. 818 g. 818 n. 163.8x31.1x22.0 ft. Sailing ship
1862 completed at Maine, USA, as STARS AND STRIPES for unknown owners. *1874* sold to H.T. Machin, Leith, and renamed NORTH STAR. *1877* purchased by C.W. Cayzer. *1878* transferred to Cayzer, Irvine and Co. *1880* sailed from Pensacola, Florida, on a voyage to Swansea with a cargo of timber and disappeared.

1. CLAN ALPINE (1) (1878–1899)
O.N. 78650. 2080 g. 1349 n. 305.6x34.8x24.2 ft.
C.2-cyl. by the shipbuilder, 250nhp, converted in *1889* to a T.3-cyl. by J. Howden and Co., Glasgow.
16.9.1878 launched by A. Stephen and Sons, Glasgow (Yard No.226) for Cayzer, Irvine and Co. *1899* sold to Dene Steam Shipping Co. Ltd. (J.T. Lunn and Co. managers), Newcastle, and renamed ELMDENE. *1903* sold to Saporta & Naar (P. Tassi manager), Italy, and renamed IDA. *1909* sold to M. Vassiliakis, Greece, and renamed SIMOPOULOS. *1909* sold to J.J. King and broken up at Gateshead.

2. CLAN FRASER (1) (1878–1895)
O.N. 80420. 2083 g. 1349 n. 305.6x34.8x24.2 ft.
C.2-cyl. by the shipbuilder, 250nhp, converted in *1889* to a T.3-cyl. by D. Rowan and Co., Glasgow.
7.11.1878 launched by A. Stephen and Sons, Glasgow (Yard No.227) for Cayzer, Irvine and Co. *1895* sold to Dene Steam Shipping Co. Ltd. (J.T. Lunn and Co. managers), Newcastle, and renamed OAKDENE. *1896* sold to A. Tagliavia & Fratelli, Italy, and renamed GIACOMO T. *1902* Renamed PRIMAVERA. *28.10.1902* wrecked on the Burlings, Portugal, whilst on a voyage from Palermo to Antwerp and Rotterdam with general cargo.

3. CLAN RANALD (1) (1878–1899)
O.N. 80439. 2068 g. 1339 n. 305.0x34.8x24.4 ft.
C.2-cyl. by D. Rowan and Co., Glasgow, 280nhp, converted in *1890* to a T.3-cyl. by A. Stephen and Sons, Glasgow.
24.12.1878 launched by A. McMillan and Son, Dumbarton (Yard No.215) for Cayzer, Irvine and Co. *1899* sold to Ranald Steamship Co. (T.P. Purdy manager), Glasgow, and renamed RANALD. *4.6.1901* foundered off Atlantic City whilst on a voyage from Trinidad to New York with general cargo.

4. CLAN GORDON (1) (1879–1897)
O.N. 80441. 2062 g. 1343 n. 305.6x34.8x24.2 ft.
C.2-cyl. by the shipbuilder, 250nhp, converted in *1888* to a T.3-cyl. by J. Howden and Co., Glasgow.
11.2.1879 launched by A. Stephen and Sons, Glasgow (Yard No.232) for Cayzer, Irvine and Co. *16.10.1897* wrecked at Umlalazi River, Zululand, whilst on a voyage from the River Clyde to Natal, Delagoa Bay and Beira with general cargo.

5. CLAN STUART (1) (1879–1900)
O.N. 80447. 2094 g. 1355 n. 305.4x34.8x24.4 ft.
C.2-cyl. by D. Rowan and Co., Glasgow, 280nhp, converted in *1889* to a T.3-cyl. by A. Stephen and Sons, Glasgow.
21.2.1879 launched by A. McMillan and Sons, Dumbarton (Yard No.216) for Cayzer, Irvine and Co. *16.2.1885* aground at Moville Point while entering Table Bay. *1900* sold to Hajee Goolam Mahomed Ajam, Bombay, and renamed RANDER REUNION. *1960* sold to Shah Steam Navigation Co. of India Ltd., Bombay, and renamed SHAH JADA. *1906* broken up at Bombay.

6. CLAN LAMONT (1) (1879–1891)
O.N. 80458. 2091 g. 1354 n. 305.6x34.8x24.2 ft.
C.2-cyl. by the shipbuilder, 250nhp, converted in *1889* to a T.3-cyl. by J. Howden and Co., Glasgow.
23.4.1879 launched by A. Stephen and Sons, Glasgow (Yard No.233) for Cayzer, Irvine and Co. *3.5.1891* wrecked off Vindiloas Point, Batticaloa, Ceylon, whilst on a voyage from Madras to London with general cargo.

7. CLAN MACDUFF (1881)
O.N. 63796. 2328 g. 1497 n. 326.1x36.1x27.7 ft.
C.2-cyl. by the shipbuilder, 200nhp.
12.10.1870 launched by Barclay, Curle and Co., Glasgow (Yard No.206) as CITY OF OXFORD for G. Smith and Sons, Glasgow. *1881* purchased by Cayzer, Irvine and Co. and renamed CLAN MACDUFF. *21.10.1881* Foundered 40 miles South of Cork whilst on a voyage from Liverpool to Bombay, 32 lives lost including the master.

8. CLAN MACLEAN (1) (1881–1903)
O.N. 63807. 2336 g. 1486 n. 326.5x36.1x27.7 ft.
C.2-cyl. by the shipbuilder, 200nhp, converted in *1893* to a T.3-cyl. by Bow, McLachlan and Co., Paisley.
10.12.1870 launched by Barclay, Curle and Co., Glasgow (Yard No.207) as CITY OF CAMBRIDGE for G. Smith and Sons, Glasgow. *1881* purchased by Cayzer, Irvine and Co. and renamed CLAN MACLEAN. *28.3.1890* struck Matamada Rock near Galle Harbour, Ceylon. *13.8.1903* wrecked 6 miles North of Cape St. Vincent whilst on a voyage from Glasgow and Liverpool to Bombay with general cargo.

9. CLAN MACLEOD (1) (1881–1884)
O.N. 63821. 2290 g. 1461 n. 325.7x36.2x27.4 ft.
C.2-cyl. by J. Howden and Co., Glasgow, 227nhp.
22.3.1871 launched by C. Connell and Co., Glasgow (Yard No.75) as CITY OF

MECCA for G. Smith and Sons, Glasgow. *1881* purchased by Cayzer, Irvine and Co. and renamed CLAN MACLEOD. *1884* sold to R.M. Sloman & Co., Germany, and renamed PROCIDA. *20.12.1900* sold to the Admiralty, London, for service as a coal hulk at Simonstown. *1901* renamed NUBIAN. *1904* renamed C.370. *1913* sold to T.W. Ward Ltd. and broken up at Morecambe.

10. CLAN MONROE (1) (1881–1897)
O.N. 85879. 2197 g. 1437 n. 285.5x37.2x24.4 ft.
C.2-cyl. by R. & W. Hawthorn, Newcastle, 300nhp, converted in *1892* to a Q.4-cyl. by Westray, Copeland and Co. Ltd., Barrow.
8.11.1881 launched by Bartram, Haswell and Co. Ltd., Sunderland (Yard No.116) for Cayzer, Irvine and Co. *1897* sold to Dene Steam Shipping Co. Ltd. (J.T. Lunn and Co., managers), Newcastle, and renamed CEDARDENE. *1899* sold to Westcott and Laurance, London. *1901* sold to Cedardene Steam Ship Co. Ltd. (Westcott and Laurance, managers), London. *24.2.1903* wrecked North of Arzile, Morocco, whilst on a voyage from the River Clyde to Alexandria.

11. CLAN MURRAY (1) (1882–1897)
O.N. 82745. 2108 g. 1373 n. 290.0x36.2x23.2 ft.
C.2-cyl. by North Eastern Marine Engineering Co., Sunderland, 250nhp, converted in 1893 to a Q.4-cyl. by Westray, Copeland and Co. Ltd., Barrow.
15.6.1881 launched by Tyne Iron Shipbuilding Co., Howdon on Tyne (Yard No.33) as MURIEL for W.B. Ritchie and Co., Dundee. *1882* purchased by Cayzer, Irvine and Co. and renamed CLAN MURRAY. *1897* sold to Dene Steam Shipping Co. Ltd. (J.T. Lunn and Co., managers), Newcastle, and renamed OLIVEDENE. *1899* sold to Lim Chin Tsong, Rangoon, and renamed SEANG LEONG. *25.7.1902* sailed from Singapore on a voyage to Amoy, China, with general cargo and disappeared.

12. CLAN MACKAY (1) (1882–1891)
O.N. 85906. 2171 g. 1423 n. 285.7x37.2x24.4 ft.
C.2-cyl. by R. & W. Hawthorn, Newcastle, 300nhp.
19.1.1882 launched by Bartram, Haswell and Co. Ltd., Sunderland (Yard No.117) for Cayzer, Irvine and Co. *9.3.1891* Wrecked on Bellicatua Rock, near Galle, Ceylon, whilst on a voyage from Madras to London.

13. CLAN MACDONALD (1) (1882–1897)
O.N. 85914. 2642 g. 1716 n. 335.5x39.3x26.9 ft.
C.2-cyl. by the shipbuilder, 400nhp.
21.2.1882 launched by Scott and Co., Greenock (Yard No.207) for Cayzer, Irvine and Co. *1897* sold to Dene Steam Shipping Co. Ltd. (J.T. Lunn and Co., managers), Newcastle, and renamed BRIARDENE. *1898* sold to Briardene Steam Ship Co. Ltd. (Anglo-American Agency Co. Ltd., managers), Newcastle. *1900* sold to Martin and Alfred Dickie, Truro, N.S. *1904* transferred to Colchester Steamship Co. Ltd. (A. Dickie manager), Lower Stewiacke, N.S. *1916* sold to Overseas Shipping Co. Ltd., Halifax, N.S. *1.12.1916* captured by the German submarine UC.19 and sunk by bombs 12 $^1/_2$ miles S.E. by S. from Bishop Rock whilst on a voyage from New York to London with general cargo.

14. CLAN CAMERON (1) (1882–1900)
O.N. 85913. 2433 g. 1585 n. 324.5x38.1x23.8 ft.
C.2-cyl. by the shipbuilder, 300nhp, and converted in *1892* to a T.3-cyl. by Naval Construction and Armaments Co. Ltd., Barrow.
22.2.1882 launched by A. Stephen and Sons, Glasgow (Yard No.261) for Cayzer, Irvine and Co. *1900* sold to Trinidad Shipping and Trading Co. Ltd. (G. Christall manager), Glasgow, and renamed MARAVAL. *1910* sold to shipbreakers.

15. CLAN BUCHANAN (1) (1882–1904)
O.N. 85927. 2933 g. 1913 n. 330.3x40.1x26.3 ft.
C.2-cyl. by D. Rowan and Co., Glasgow, 400nhp, converted in *1899* to a T.3-cyl. by Vickers, Sons and Maxim Ltd., Barrow.
22.2.1882 launched by A. McMillan and Son, Dumbarton (Yard No.237) for Cayzer, Irvine and Co. *1904* sold to Essajee Tajbhoy, Bombay, and renamed SHAH ALLUM. *1907* sold to Shah Steam Navigation Co. of India Ltd., Bombay. *1908* sold to Hajee Ahmad Hassum, Bombay. *10.6.1909* wrecked at Piram Island, near Gogha, whilst on a voyage from Rangoon to Bhavnagar, W. India.

16. CLAN GRAHAM (1) (1882–1905)
O.N. 85943. 2926 g. 1911 n. 330.5x40.2x26.3 ft.
C.2-cyl. by D. Rowan and Co., Glasgow, 400nhp, converted in *1894* to a T.3-cyl. by Naval Construction and Armaments Co. Ltd., Barrow.
21.3.1882 launched by Napier, Shanks and Bell, Glasgow (Yard No.14) for Cayzer, Irvine and Co. *1905* sold to Bombay and Persia Steam Navigation Co. Ltd., Bombay and renamed MAJIDI. *1912* sold to Comm. Tomaso Astarita, Italy, and renamed MARIA VITTORIA. *1913* Renamed MARIA DELLE VITTORIE. *4.6.1915* last reported arrival at Naples from Norfolk, Virginia, via Gibraltar, laid-up at Naples. *1916* Scrapped at Naples.

17. CLAN MACKENZIE (1) (1882–1904)
O.N. 85944. 2954 g. 1930 n. 329.6x40.2x26.3 ft.
C.2-cyl. by D. Rowan and Co., Glasgow, 400nhp, converted in *1898* to a T.3-cyl. by Vickers, Sons and Maxim Ltd., Barrow.
20.4.1882 launched by Ramage and Ferguson, Leith (Yard No.35) for Cayzer, Irvine and Co. *1904* sold to Essajee Tajbhoy, Bombay, and renamed SHAH AMEER. *1907* sold to Shah Steam Navigation Co. of India Ltd., Bombay. *1908* sold to Hajee Ahmad Hassum, Bombay. *1909* sold to Bombay and Hujaz Steam Navigation Co. of India Ltd., Bombay. *1912* sold to shipbreakers at Bombay.

18. CLAN DRUMMOND (1882–1898)
O.N. 86669. 2922 g. 1904 n. 330.3x40.1x26.3 ft.
C.2-cyl. by D. Rowan and Co., Glasgow, 400nhp, converted in *1893* to a T.3-cyl. by Naval Construction and Armaments Co. Ltd., Barrow.
5.1882 launched by A. McMillan and Son, Dumbarton (Yard No.238) for Cayzer, Irvine and Co. *10.1.1891* in collision with steamer ANDORRA and barque SIR ROBERT FERNIE in River Hooghly. *28.1.1898* foundered in the Bay of Biscay whilst on a voyage from the River Clyde and Liverpool to Algoa with general cargo. The master and 36 crew were lost.

19. CLAN CAMPBELL (1) (1882)
O.N. 86663. 2434 g. 1585 n. 324.5x38.1x23.8 ft.
C.2-cyl. by the shipbuilder, 300nhp.
5.6.1882 launched by A. Stephen and Sons, Glasgow (Yard No.262) for Cayzer, Irvine and Co. *22.9.1882* wrecked at Bail du Cap, Mauritius, whilst on her maiden voyage. Salvage attempts had been delayed by quarantine restrictions.

20. CLAN MACGREGOR (1) (1882–1899)
O.N. 86692. 2956 g. 1927 n. 329.6x40.3x26.4 ft.
C.2-cyl. by D. Rowan and Co., Glasgow, 400nhp, converted in 1898 to a T.3-cyl. by Vickers, Sons and Maxim Ltd., Barrow.
29.7.1882 launched by Ramage and Ferguson, Leith (Yard No.36) for Cayzer, Irvine and Co. *4.9.1899* Sank off Cape St. Vincent following a collision with the Danish steamer CATHAY, 4111/98 whilst on a voyage from Madras to London.

21. CLAN FORBES (1) (1882–1903)
O.N. 86680. 2441 g. 1591 n. 324.5x38.1x23.8 ft.
C.2-cyl. by the Shipbuilder, 350nhp, converted in *1892* to a T.3-cyl. by Westray, Copeland and Co. Ltd., Barrow.
15.8.1882 launched by A. Stephen and Sons, Glasgow (Yard No.263) for Cayzer, Irvine and Co. *1903* sold to Furness, Withy and Co. Ltd., West Hartlepool, and renamed LONDON CITY. *1910* sold to Denaby and Cadeby Main Collieries Ltd., London. *1920* transferred to Denaby Shipping and Commercial Co. Ltd., London. *1922* sold to German shipbreakers.

22. CLAN SINCLAIR (1) (1882–1905)
O.N. 86705. 2933 g. 1912 n. 330.5x40.2x26.3 ft.
C.2-cyl. by D. Rowan and Co., Glasgow, 400nhp, converted in *1897* to a T.3-cyl. by Naval Construction and Armaments Co. Ltd., Barrow.
15.8.1882 launched by Napier, Shanks and Bell, Glasgow (Yard No.15) for Cayzer, Irvine and Co. *1905* sold to Bombay and Persia Steam Navigation Co. Ltd., Bombay, and renamed RAHMANI. *20.7.1917* sank following a collision in the Mediterranean Sea whilst on a voyage from Bombay to Genoa.

23. CLAN OGILVIE (1882–1888)
O.N. 86718. 2425 g. 1584 n. 324.5x38.1x23.8 ft.
C.2-cyl. by the shipbuilder, 300nhp.
24.11.1882 launched by A. Stephen and Sons, Glasgow (Yard No.264) for Cayzer, Irvine and Co. *27.1.1883* in collision with steamer INFLEXIBLE in Bombay Harbour. *8.1.1888* wrecked in the Straits of Bonifacio, Corsica whilst on a voyage from Bombay to Marseilles.

24. CLAN GRANT (1) (1883–1900)
O.N. 86745. 3545 g. 2306 n. 350.5x41.1x26.6 ft.
C.2-cyl. by the shipbuilder, 400nhp.
24.1.1883 launched by A. Stephen and Son, Glasgow (Yard No.272) as PROCIDA for R.M. Sloman & Co., Germany. Sold whilst fitting out to Cayzer, Irvine and Co. and completed as CLAN GRANT. *1900* sold to Pacific Whaling & Fishery Joint Stock Co of Count H.H. Keyserling & Co., Russia, and renamed MICHAIL. *1905* taken

over by the Japanese Government (Department of Agriculture & Commerce) and renamed MIHAIRU MARU. *1914* sold to Ishikari Sekitan Kabushiki Kaisha, Japan, and renamed MIHARU MARU. *1923* sold to Hokkaido Tanko Kisen Kaisha, Japan. *1927* sold to Sugaya Kabushiki Kaisha, Japan. *1929* sold to Japanese shipbreakers.

25. CLAN MACARTHUR (1) (1883–1904)
O.N. 87657. 3984 g. 2635 n. 381.2x43.3x27.9 ft.
C.2-cyl. by the Shipbuilder, 475nhp, converted in *1893* to a T.3-cyl. by Naval Construction and Armaments Co. Ltd., Barrow.
12.3.1883 launched by Mrs Arthur at Scott and Co., Greenock (Yard No.223) for Cayzer, Irvine and Co. *1904* sold to Essajee Tajbhoy, Bombay, and renamed SHAH JEHAN. *1907* sold to Shah Steam Navigation Co. of India Ltd., Bombay. *1909* sold to Bombay and Hujaz Steam Navigation Co. of India Ltd., Bombay. *1912* sold to shipbreakers at Bombay.

26. CLAN MACPHERSON (1) (1883–1905)
O.N. 87709. 3921 g. 2587 n. 380.7x43.2x28.3 ft.
C.2-cyl. by D. Rowan and Co., Glasgow, 475nhp, converted in *1892* to a T.3-cyl. by D. & W. Henderson & Co. Ltd., Glasgow.
25.5.1883 launched by Napier, Shanks and Bell, Glasgow (Yard No.20) for Cayzer, Irvine and Co. *1905* sold to Max Jebsen, Germany, and renamed HANNA. *1905* sold to Gustav Diederichsen, Germany. *1906* sold to Max Jebsen, Germany. *1906* sold to Kishimoto Kisen Kabushiki Kaisha, Japan, and renamed SHINKOKU MARU. *1914* sold to shipbreakers.

27. CLAN MACINTOSH (1) (1883–1905)
O.N. 87690. 3985 g. 2636 n. 381.2x43.3x27.9 ft.
C.2-cyl. by the shipbuilder, 475nhp, converted in *1892* to a T.3-cyl. by Naval Construction and Armaments Co. Ltd., Barrow.
6.6.1883 launched by Scott and Co., Greenock (Yard No.224) for Cayzer, Irvine and Co. *29.11.1885* in collision with barque FIDELIO near the Royal Sovereign Light Vessel on a voyage from London to Glasgow with general cargo. *1905* sold to Max Jebsen, Germany, and renamed TOTTI. *1905* sold to Gustav Diederichsen, Germany. *1906* sold to Max Jebsen, Germany. *1907* sold to Madras Steam Navigation Co. Ltd., Rangoon, and renamed CLAN MACINTOSH. *1914* sold to shipbreakers.

28. CLAN MATHESON (1) (1883–1905)
O.N. 87725. 3917 g. 2581 n. 380.7x43.2x28.3 ft.
C.2-cyl by D. Rowan and Co., Glasgow, 475nhp, who converted it to a T.3-cyl. in 1892.
20.8.1883 launched by Napier, Shanks and Bell, Glasgow (Yard No.21) for Cayzer, Irvine and Co. *12.1893* ashore in the Suez Canal, refloated. *1905* sold to Max Jebsen, Germany, and renamed MARIECHEN. *1905* sold to Gustav Diederichsen, Germany. *1906* sold to Max Jebsen, Germany. *24.1.1906* stranded at Chichagoff, Alaska, whilst on a voyage from San Francisco to Vladivostok. Subsequently refloated and towed to Seattle where she was partly dismantled and sunk in the harbour.

29. CLAN MACNEIL (1) (1891–1902)
O.N. 98611. 2519 g. 1591 n. 312.0x39.0x23.5 ft.
T.3-cyl. by the shipbuilder, 300nhp.
14.2.1891 launched and *3.1891* completed by W. Doxford and Sons Ltd., Sunderland (Yard No.203) for The Clan Line Steamers Ltd. *1902* sold to Ellerman Lines Ltd. (F. Swift, later Graham Smith manager), Liverpool, and renamed BELGRAVIAN. *1922* sold to Kenneth Saunders, London. *1929* sold to Italian shipbreakers.

30. CLAN MACLEOD (2) (1891–1902)
O.N. 98620. 2517 g. 1589 n. 312.0x39.0x23.5 ft.
T.3-cyl by the shipbuilder, 300nhp.
25.3.1891 launched and *5.1891* completed by W. Doxford and Sons Ltd., Sunderland (Yard No.204) for The Clan Line Steamers Ltd. *1902* sold to Ellerman Lines Ltd. (F. Swift, later Graham Smith manager), Liverpool, and renamed BOSNIAN. *1922* sold to M. Basiliades, Greece, and renamed PSARA. *1929* sold to shipbreakers.

31. CLAN MACKINNON (1) (1891–1902)
O.N. 98627. 2268 g. 1473 n. 305.0x39.0x23.3 ft.
T.3-cyl. by the shipbuilder, 300nhp.
21.4.1891 launched and *5.1891* completed by A. Stephen and Sons, Glasgow (Yard No.332) for The Clan Line Steamers Ltd. *1902* sold to Furness, Withy and Co. Ltd., West Hartlepool, and renamed EVANGELINE. *1911* sold to A. Embiricos, Greece, and renamed PELAGOS. *14.8.1912* stranded off Barry. Subsequently refloated but found to be badly damaged. Sold to T.W. Ward Ltd. and broken up at Morecambe.

32. CLAN MACINTYRE (1) (1891–1902)
O.N. 98636. 2514 g. 1590 n. 312.0x39.0x23.5 ft.
T.3-cyl. by the shipbuilder, 300nhp.
28.4.1891 launched and *6.1891* completed by W. Doxford and Sons Ltd., Sunderland (Yard No.205) for The Clan Line Steamers Ltd. *1902* sold to Ellerman Lines Ltd. (F. Swift manager), Liverpool, and renamed BULGARIAN. *20.1.1917* torpedoed and sunk in the North Atlantic by the German submarine U84 whilst on a voyage from Cartagena to Garston with a cargo of iron ore. The master and 13 crew were lost and a further 9 crew were taken prisoner.

33. CLAN MACNAB (1) (1891–1902)
O.N. 98645. 2268 g. 1473 n. 305.0x39.0x23.3 ft.
T.3-cyl. by the shipbuilder, 300nhp.
9.6.1891 launched by Miss Constance Cayzer and *6.1891* completed by A. Stephen and Sons, Glasgow (Yard No.333) for The Clan Line Steamers Ltd. *23.12.1894* in collision with Russian gunboat GREMIATSCHY in the Suez Canal. *1902* sold to Furness, Withy and Co. Ltd., West Hartlepool, and renamed ST. JOHN CITY. *1910* sold to Anglo Hellenic Steamship Co. (A.A. Embiricos manager), Greece, and renamed PONTOS. *1913* sold to T.N. Caruso, Greece. *1915* Requisitioned by the Admiralty and scuttled as a blockship at Scapa Flow. *1922* raised and broken up.

34. CLAN MACALISTER (1) (1891–1902)
O.N. 98662. 2268 g. 1436 n. 305.0x39.0x23.3 ft.
T.3-cyl. by shipbuilder, 300nhp.
5.8.1891 launched and *8.1891* completed by A. Stephen and Sons, Glasgow (Yard No.334) for The Clan Line Steamers Ltd. *1902* sold to Furness, Withy and Co. Ltd., West Hartlepool, and renamed LOYALIST. *27.9.1904* wrecked at Freshwater Cove, Trepassey Bay, Newfoundland, whilst on a voyage from Halifax N.S. to London with general cargo.

35. CLAN ROSS (1) (1894–1914)
O.N. 104539. 2602 g. 1664 n. 312.0x40.2x24.7 ft.
T.3-cyl. by the shipbuilder, 317nhp.
7.6.1894 launched and *7.1894* completed by Naval Construction and Armaments Co. Ltd., Barrow (Yard No.227) for The Clan Line Steamers Ltd. *1914* sold to The Adelaide Steam Ship Co. Ltd., Newcastle, N.S.W., and renamed CANTARA. *1924* sold to South China Steam Ship Co., China, and renamed HWAH CHENG. *1928* sold to Yee Cheong & Co., China. *1930* sold to shipbreakers.

36. CLAN CAMPBELL (2) (1894–1914)
O.N. 104576. 2600 g. 1662 n. 312.0x40.2x24.7 ft.
T.3-cyl. by the shipbuilder, 317nhp.
3.9.1894 launched and *10.1894* completed by Naval Construction and Armaments Co. Ltd., Barrow (Yard No.228) for The Clan Line Steamers Ltd. *1914* sold to The Adelaide Steam Ship Co. Ltd., Newcastle, N.S.W., and renamed CAMIRA. *1925* sold to W. McBain, China, and renamed YUNG NING. *1927* sold to Cie. Extreme Orientale, France. *1928* sold to Louis Dubest (Alex Gerondal manager), France, and renamed COMMANDANT HENRI RIVIERE. *1936* sold to Shiu Tsing Hong (Far East Shipping Co. Ltd., managers), China. *12.1941* sunk by Japanese forces while lying at Canton.

37. CLAN MACKAY (2) (1894–1914)
O.N. 104593. 2600 g. 1654 n. 312.0x40.2x24.7 ft.
T.3-cyl. by the shipbuilder, 317nhp.
31.10.1894 launched and *12.1894* completed by Naval Construction and Armaments Co. Ltd., Barrow (Yard No.229) for The Clan Line Steamers Ltd. *1914* sold to The Adelaide Steam Ship Co. Ltd., Newcastle, N.S.W., and renamed CEDUNA. *1925* sold to Woo Kuei Fen (Tung, Tuck & Co., managers), China, and renamed TUNG-TUCK. *1937* sold to Lee Yuan Steamship Co., China, and renamed CHANG TEH. *1938* sold to J.D. Tsounias (China Hellenic Lines Ltd., managers), Greece, and renamed PANANIS. *1941* seized by Japanese forces and subsequently became a war loss.

38. CLAN MACRAE (1) (1894–1899)
O.S. 99099. 2605 g. 1664 n. 305.0x41.1x18.8 ft.
T.3-cyl. by North Eastern Marine Engineering Co. Ltd., Sunderland.
13.5.1892 launched and *6.1892* completed by J. Blumer and Co., Sunderland (Yard No.122) as SHAT EL ARAB for Persian Gulf Steam Ship Co. Ltd., London. *1894* purchased by The Clan Line Steamers Ltd. and renamed CLAN MACRAE. *16.5.1899* sold to Chadwick Steam Ship Co. Ltd. (R.B. Avery manager), Newcastle, and renamed CARMELITE. *1916* sold to Berg and Co. (M. Ramet manager),

London. *1916* sold to Page Shipping Co. Ltd. (Hopkins, Jones and Co. Ltd., managers), Cardiff. *1917* management transferred to John I. Jacobs and Co. *2.3.1918* torpedoed and sunk 10 miles S.W. by W. from the Calf of Man by the German submarine U105 whilst on a voyage from Bilbao to Cardiff with a cargo of iron ore. Two members of the crew were lost.

39. AMARA (1894–1895)
O.N. 98197. 2454 g. 1566 n. 289.5x40.3x16.8 ft.
T.3-cyl. by North Eastern Marine Engineering Co. Ltd., Sunderland, 248nhp.
15.11.1890 launched and *1.1891* completed by J. Blumer and Co., Sunderland (Yard No.108) as AMARA for Persian Gulf Steam Ship Co. Ltd., London. *1894* purchased by The Clan Line Steamers Ltd. *1895* sold to W. Keswick, Glasgow. *17.7.1896* sold to Indo-China Steam Navigation Co. Ltd., London. *1911* sold to O. Aso, Japan, and renamed TAGA MARU. *1918* sold to Fukugawa Ringyo Kabushiki Kaisha, Japan. *1920* owners restyled as Fukugawa Kisen Kabushiki Kaisha. *1922* sold to Tajima Nobukazu, Japan. *12.3.1925* wrecked off Ichiyezaki Wakayama.

40. TIGRIS (1894–1895)
O.S. 98167. 2412 g. 1536 n. 290.0x40.1x16.8 ft.
T.3-cyl. by North Eastern Marine Engineering Co. Ltd., Sunderland, 220nhp.
30.8.1890 launched and *9.1890* completed by J. Blumer and Co., Sunderland (Yard No.107) as TIGRIS for Persian Gulf Steam Ship Co. Ltd., London, *1894* purchased by The Clan Line Steamers Ltd. *1895* sold to W. Keswick, Glasgow. *17.7.1896* sold to Indo-China Steam Navigation Co. Ltd., London, and renamed HIN SANG. *1910* sold to S. Yamaki, Japan, and renamed KAIHEI MARU. *21.7.1911* wrecked in Soya Strait, Japan.

41. GORJI (1894–1895)
O.N. 87156. 1710 g. 1111 n. 255.5x35.1x24.5 ft.
C.2-cyl. by the shipbuilder, 195nhp.
7.1883 launched by Wigham Richardson and Co., Newcastle (Yard No.157) as GORJI for Persian Gulf Steam Ship Co. Ltd., London. *1894* purchased by The Clan Line Steamers Ltd. *1895* sold to Bombay & Persia S.N. Co. Ltd., London, and renamed MOSHTARI. *1914* sold to Abe Shokei, Dairen, Japan, and renamed FUKUJU MARU. *1916* sold to Murao Kisen Goshi Kaisha, Amagasaki, Japan, name unchanged. *3.3.1930* wrecked near Shiriyasaki on passage Ofunato to Muroran.

42. CLAN MENZIES (1) (1896–1925)
O.N. 105979. 2669 g. 1704 n. 312.3x40.2x23.5 ft.
T.3-cyl by the shipbuilder, 317nhp.
1.2.1896 launched and *2.1896* completed by Naval Construction and Armaments Co. Ltd., Barrow (Yard No.245) for The Clan Line Steamers Ltd. *1925* sold to A. Ardito, Italy, and renamed NOSTRA SIGNORA DI CORONATA. *1928* broken up in Italy.

43. CLAN LINDSAY (1) (1896–1898)
O.N. 105997. 2668 g. 1705 n. 312.3x40.2x23.5 ft.
T.3-cyl. by shipbuilder, 330nhp.
2.4.1896 launched and *4.1896* completed by Naval Construction and Armaments

Co. Ltd., Barrow (Yard No.246) for The Clan Line Steamers Ltd. *21.3.1898* wrecked at Mazeppa Bay, North of the Great Kei River, Cape Colony, whilst on a voyage from the River Clyde and Liverpool to Mauritius.

44. CLAN CHISHOLM (1) (1896–1925)
O.N. 106107. 2647 g. 1681 n. 312.5x40.2x23.5 ft.
T.3-cyl. by the shipbuilder, 313nhp.
29.6.1896 launched and *7.1896* completed by A. Stephen and Sons, Glasgow (Yard No.366) for The Clan Line Steamers Ltd. *18.9.1916* chased by a submarine in the Mediterranean Sea and escaped. *13.11.1916* attacked by gunfire from a submarine at the entrance to the English Channel and escaped. *1925* sold to Nippon Kaiun K.K., Japan, and renamed FUKKO MARU. *7.2.1926* wrecked at Katsuura whilst on a voyage from Muroran to Yokohama with a cargo of coal.

45. CLAN OGILVY (1) (1896–1913)
O.N. 106030. 2677 g. 1683 n. 312.5x40.2x23.5 ft.
T.3-cyl. by the shipbuilder, 313nhp.
25.8.1896 launched and *9.1896* completed by A. Stephen and Sons, Glasgow (Yard No.367) for The Clan Line Steamers Ltd. *1913* sold to U. Iwaki, Japan, and renamed TAIYO MARU. *1918* sold to Hamaguchi Kisen Kabushiki Kaisha, Japan, *1925* sold to Taiyo Kisen Goshi Kaisha, Japan. *1929* sold to Sovtorgflot, Russia, and renamed PERVI KRABOLOV and converted into a crab cannery. *1965* deleted from Lloyd's Register in the absence of any report of the vessel since 1955.

46. CLAN SUTHERLAND (1) (1896–1922)
O.N. 106037. 2820 g. 1810 n. 326.0x40.2x23.5 ft.
T.3-cyl. by the shipbuilder, 317nhp.
26.9.1896 launched and *10.1896* completed by Naval Construction and Armaments Co. Ltd., Barrow (Yard No.252) for The Clan Line Steamers Ltd. *17.4.1917* torpedoed and damaged by a German submarine 18 miles S.E. of Start Point whilst on a voyage from Cochin to London and beached at Dartmouth. Subsequently refloated and repaired. *1922* sold to Sato Shokai Goshi Kaisha (T. Sato & Co., managers), Japan, and renamed SHINSHU MARU. *1924* sold to Azuma Kisen Goshi Kaisha. *1933* sold to Japanese shipbreakers.

47. IMPERIALIST/CLAN SHAW (1) (1896–1898)
O.N. 106016. 3442 g. 2177 n. 340.2x45.6x24.5 ft. Turret Deck Steamer
T.3-cyl. by the shipbuilder, 300nhp.
25.4.1896 launched and *7.1896* completed by W. Doxford and Sons Ltd., Sunderland (Yard No.242) as IMPERIALIST for Angier Brothers, London. *1896* purchased by The Clan Line Steamers Ltd. *1898* renamed CLAN SHAW. *1898* sold to Nautilus Steam Shipping Co. Ltd. (F. and W. Ritson, managers), Sunderland, and renamed VINE BRANCH. *23.3.1917* sailed from Dakar on a voyage to Liverpool with a cargo of nitrates and disappeared. She was presumed to have been torpedoed and sunk about *11.4.1917* with the loss of her crew of 44.

48. BULLIONIST (1896–1898)
O.N. 106021. 3435 g. 2196 n. 340.3x45.6x24.5 ft. Turret Deck Steamer
T.3-cyl by the shipbuilder, 274nhp.

27.6.1896 launched and *8.1896* completed by W. Doxford and Sons Ltd., Sunderland (Yard No.243) as BULLIONIST for Angier Brothers, London. *1896* purchased by The Clan Line Steamers Ltd. *17.9.1898* sold to Nautilus Steam Shipping Co. Ltd. (F. and W. Ritson, managers), Sunderland and renamed ORANGE BRANCH. *11.1919* sold to "K" Steamship Co. Ltd. (Kaye, Son and Co. Ltd., managers), London and renamed KEMMEL. *23.2.1920* wrecked at St. Vincent, Cape Verde Islands whilst on a voyage from Rosario to Constantinople with a cargo of meat and flour.

49. CLAN MACDONALD (2) (1897–1922)
O.N. 106067. 4839 g. 3113 n. 400.6x50.2x27.7 ft. Turret Deck Steamer
T.3-cyl. by the shipbuilder, 413nhp.
3.3.1897 launched and *4.1897* completed by W. Doxford and Sons Ltd., Sunderland (Yard No.250) for The Clan Line Steamers Ltd. *12.1897* in collision with steamer OBRA, owned by British India Steam Navigation Co., at Garden House Point in River Hooghly on a voyage from UK to Calcutta with general cargo. *1922* sold to Hokuyo Kisen Kabushiki Kaisha, Japan and renamed HOKUYO MARU. *1928* sold to shipbreakers.

50. CLAN MURRAY (2) (1897–1917)
O.N. 106077. 4839 g. 3121 n. 400.0x50.2x27.8 ft. Turret Deck Steamer
T.3-cyl. by the shipbuilder, 413nhp.
17.4.1897 launched and *5.1897* completed by W. Doxford and Sons Ltd., Sunderland (Yard No.251) for The Clan Line Steamers Ltd. *29.5.1917* torpedoed and sunk 40 miles S.W. of the Fastnet by the Germany submarine UC.55 whilst on a voyage from Port Pirie to Belfast with a cargo of wheat. Sixty four members of the crew were lost.

51. CLAN MONROE (2) (1897–1905)
O.N. 106097. 4853 g. 3121 n. 400.1x50.2x27.8 ft. Turret Deck Steamer
T.3-cyl. by the shipbuilder, 413nhp.
3.6.1897 launched and *7.1897* completed by W. Doxford and Sons Ltd., Sunderland (Yard No.254) for The Clan Line Steamers Ltd. *1.7.1905* wrecked at Slangkop Point, Cape Peninsula whilst on a voyage from Glasgow and Liverpool to South African ports with general cargo.

52. CLAN ROBERTSON (1) (1897–1922)
O.N. 108684. 4839 g. 3104 n. 400.2x50.2x27.7 ft. Turret Deck Steamer
T.3-cyl. by the shipbuilder, 413nhp.
17.7.1897 launched and *9.1897* completed by W. Doxford and Sons Ltd., Sunderland (Yard No.255) for The Clan Line Steamers Ltd. *20.6.1915* chased by a submarine in St. George's Channel and escaped. *1922* sold to Kyosei Kisen Kabushiki Kaisha, Japan, and renamed KYOSEI MARU. *6.1.1924* Foundered South of the Aleutian Islands whilst on a voyage from Victoria B.C. to Yokohama with a cargo of lumber and wheat.

53. CLAN MACFARLANE (1) (1898–1915)
O.N. 108742. 4823 g. 3107 n. 400.5x50.2x27.6 ft. Turret Deck Steamer
T.3-cyl by the shipbuilder, 413nhp.

6.3.1898 launched and *4.1898* completed by W. Doxford and Sons Ltd., Sunderland (Yard No.261) for The Clan Line Steamers Ltd. *30.12.1915* torpedoed and sunk 66 miles S.E. of E from Cape Martello, Crete, by the German submarine U38 with the loss of 52 members of the crew. She was on a voyage from Liverpool to Bombay with general cargo.

54. CLAN FERGUSON (1) (1898–1917)
O.N. 108779. 4808 g. 3107 n. 400.6x50.2x27.5 ft. Turret Deck Steamer
T.3-cyl. by the shipbuilder, 413nhp.
4.10.1898 launched by Vickers, Sons and Maxim Ltd., Barrow (Yard No.267) for The Clan Line Steamers Ltd. *6.9.1917* torpedoed and sunk 15 miles N.W. from Cape Spartel by the German submarine UB.49 whilst on a voyage from the River Clyde to Bombay with coal and general cargo. Ten members of the crew were lost.

55. CLAN CUMMING (1) (1899–1925)
O.N. 108797. 4808 g. 3108 n. 400.6x50.2x27.5 ft. Turret Deck Steamer
T.3-cyl. by the shipbuilder, 413nhp.
26.1.1899 launched by Vickers, Sons and Maxim Ltd., Barrow (Yard No.268) for The Clan Line Steamers Ltd. *5.11.1917* torpedoed and damaged by a German submarine 20 miles S.W. of the Lizard whilst on a voyage from Baltimore to Brest with a cargo of copper, steel and timber. Towed to Falmouth and beached. Subsequently refloated, repaired and returned to service. *1925* sold to Soc. Anon. Cantiere Olivo, Italy, and renamed ETTORE. *1927* sold to Tito Campanella S.A., Italy, and renamed ELISA CAMPANELLA. *1932* sold to shipbreakers.

56. CLAN MACAULAY (1) (1899–1929)
O.N. 108800. 2834 g. 1775 n. 326.0x40.2x23.6 ft.
T.3-cyl. by the shipbuilder, 313nhp.
27.2.1899 launched by Mrs Joss and *4.1899* completed by A. Stephen and Sons, Glasgow (Yard No.381) for The Clan Line Steamers Ltd. *1929* sold to Alloa Shipbreaking Co. Ltd. and broken up at Alloa.

57. CLAN COLQUHOUN (1) (1899–1925)
O.N. 111187. 5856 g. 3760 n. 440.0x51.6x28.9 ft. Turret Deck Steamer
T.3-cyl. by the shipbuilder, 436nhp.
11.3.1899 launched and *4.1899* completed by W. Doxford and Sons Ltd., Sunderland (Yard No.269) for The Clan Line Steamers Ltd. *25.11.1916* attacked by gunfire from a submarine in the Mediterranean Sea and escaped. *1925* sold to Villain & Fassio, Italy, and renamed NASCO. *1927* sold to Soc. Anon. Parodi & Corrado, Italy, and renamed CENGIO. *1929* sold to Italian shipbreakers.

58. CLAN MACLAREN (1) (1899–1924)
O.N. 111188. 2832 g. 1775 n. 326.0x40.2x23.6 ft.
T.3-cyl. by the shipbuilder, 313nhp.
24.4.1899 launched by Mrs J. Maclaren and *6.1899* completed by A. Stephen and Sons, Glasgow (Yard No.382) for The Clan Line Steamers Ltd. *20.6.1918* attacked by a submarine in the Atlantic Ocean and escaped when the torpedo missed. *1924* sold to Kuribayashi Shosen K.K., Japan, and renamed MURORAN MARU No.6. *1933* sold to shipbreakers.

59. CLAN FARQUHAR (1) (1899–1917)
O.N. 111209. 5858 g. 3757 n. 439.0x51.6x28.9 ft. Turret Deck Steamer
T.3-cyl. by the shipbuilder, 436nhp.
24.6.1899 launched and *7.1899* completed by W. Doxford and Sons Ltd., Sunderland (Yard No.271) for The Clan Line Steamers Ltd. *26.2.1917* torpedoed and sunk 80 miles North of Benghazi by the German submarine UB.43 whilst on a voyage from Calcutta to London with general cargo. Forty nine members of the crew were lost and the second engineer was taken prisoner.

60. CLAN MACFADYEN (1) (1899–1921)
O.N. 111220. 2816 g. 1755 n. 326.2x40.2x23.5 ft.
T.3-cyl. by the shipbuilder, 317nhp.
9.8.1899 launched and *9.1899* completed by Blackwood and Gordon, Port Glasgow (Yard No.241) for The Clan Line Steamers Ltd. *2.5.1916* attacked by gunfire from a submarine in the Bay of Biscay whilst on a voyage from Mauritius to London with general cargo and escaped. *1921* sold to Yamamoto Shoji K.K., Japan, and renamed SHUNKA MARU. *1924* renamed SHINKA MARU. *1926* reverted to SHUNKA MARU. *19.7.1932* sank after striking a rock whilst on a voyage from Tsingtao to Chemulpo, Korea.

61. CLAN URQUHART (1) (1899–1929)
O.N. 111219. 5855 g. 3757 n. 440.0x51.6x28.9 ft. Turret Deck Steamer
T.3-cyl. by the shipbuilder, 435nhp.
22.8.1899 launched and *9.1899* completed by W. Doxford and Sons Ltd., Sunderland (Yard No.272) for The Clan Line Steamers Ltd. *1929* sold to Emil R. Retzlaff, Germany, for £12,000 and renamed GENERALDIREKTOR SONNENSCHEIN. *1931* sold to W. Kunstmann, Germany. *1933* broken up at Stettin by Stettiner Oderwerke A.G.

62. CLAN ALPINE (2) (1899–1917)
O.N. 111232. 3587 g. 2285 n. 355.0x45.6x24.7 ft. Turret Deck Steamer
T.3-cyl. by the shipbuilder, 330nhp.
22.9.1899 launched and *10.1899* completed by W. Doxford and Sons Ltd., Sunderland (Yard No.273) for The Clan Line Steamers Ltd. *9.6.1917* torpedoed and sunk 40 miles N.E. $1/2$ E. from Muckle Flugga by the German submarine U60 whilst on a voyage from the River Tyne to Archangel. Eight members of the crew were lost.

63. CLAN MACLACHLAN (1) (1900–1917)
O.N. 111252. 4729 g. 3008 n. 395.3x48.0x27.1 ft.
T.3-cyl. by the shipbuilder, 400nhp.
20.2.1900 launched and *4.1900* completed by A. Stephen and Sons, Glasgow (Yard No.385) for The Clan Line Steamers Ltd. *19.7.1917* sank 60 miles S.W. of Cape Spartel following a collision with the Italian steamer EUROPA, 7870/07 whilst on a voyage from Cardiff to Gibraltar with general cargo. The third engineer and five lascars were lost.

64. CLAN FRASER (2) (1900–1919)
O.N. 111259. 3588 g. 2285 n. 355.0x45.6x24.7 ft. Turret Deck Steamer
T.3-cyl. by the shipbuilder, 330nhp.
30.3.1900 launched and *5.1900* completed by W. Doxford and Sons Ltd., Sunderland (Yard No.276) for The Clan Line Steamers Ltd. *1919* sold to A.S. & A.G. Coutsodontis, Greece, and renamed AGHIA PARASKEVI. *20.2.1920* Foundered off Cape St. Thomas, Brazil, whilst on a voyage from Buenos Aires to Malta with a cargo of flour and coal.

65. CLAN GORDON (2) (1900–1919)
O.N. 111269. 3589 g. 2286 n. 355.0x45.6x24.7 ft. Turret Deck Steamer
T.3-cyl. by the Shipbuilder, 330nhp.
12.5.1900 launched and *6.1900* completed by W. Doxford and Sons Ltd., Sunderland (Yard No.277) for The Clan Line Steamers Ltd. *30.7.1919* capsized and sank 140 miles S.E. of Cape Hatteras whilst on a voyage from New York to Dairen via the Panama Canal with a cargo of case oil and wax.

66. CLAN LAMONT (2) (1900–1928)
O.N. 111280. 3594 g. 2286 n. 355.0x45.6x24.7 ft. Turret Deck Steamer
T.3-cyl. by the shipbuilder, 330nhp.
16.6.1900 launched and *7.1900* completed by W. Doxford and Sons Ltd., Sunderland (Yard No.278) for The Clan Line Steamers Ltd. *3.9.1928* towed into Port Elizabeth with engine defects by New Zealand Shipping Company PAPIPAKI 7166/14. *12.1928* sold to P. & W. MacLellan Ltd. for £5,500 and broken up at Bo'ness.

67. CLAN RANALD (2) (1900–1909)
O.N. 111290. 3596 g. 2285 n. 355.0x45.6x24.7 ft. Turret Deck Steamer
T.3-cyl. by the shipbuilder, 330nhp.
31.7.1900 launched and *9.1900* completed by W. Doxford and Sons Ltd., Sunderland (Yard No.279) for The Clan Line Steamers Ltd. *31.1.1909* capsized and sank off Edithburgh, South Australia, whilst on a voyage from Adelaide to Durban, East London and Capetown with a cargo of flour and wheat.

68. CLAN STUART (2) (1900–1914)
O.N. 113911. 3594 g. 2285 n. 355.0x45.6x24.7 ft. Turret Deck Steamer
T.3-cyl. by the shipbuilder, 330nhp.
8.9.1900 launched and *10.1900* completed by W. Doxford and Sons Ltd., Sunderland (Yard No.280) for The Clan Line Steamers Ltd. *21.11.1914* wrecked at Simons Bay, Cape Colony, after arriving at Capetown from the United Kingdom.

69. CLAN MACRAE (2) / CLAN CAMERON (2) (1900–1917)
O.N. 113919. 3595 g. 2285 n. 355.0x45.6x24.7 ft. Turret Deck Steamer
T.3-cyl. by the shipbuilder, 330nhp.
11.10.1900 launched as CLAN MACRAE and *11.1900* completed by W. Doxford and Sons Ltd., Sunderland (Yard No.281) for The Clan Line Steamers Ltd. as CLAN CAMERON. *22.12.1917* torpedoed and sunk 23 miles S.W. by S. $^1/_2$ S. from Portland Bill by the German submarine UB.58 whilst on a voyage from Chittagong to London with a cargo of tea and jute.

70. CLAN MACMILLAN (1) (1901–1917)
O.N. 113992. 4525 g. 2805 n. 396.5x48.2x27.0 ft.
T.3-cyl. by Greenock Foundry Co., Greenock, 398nhp.
16.10.1901 launched and *12.1901* completed by A. McMillan and Son Ltd., Dumbarton (Yard No.380) for The Clan Line Steamers Ltd. *23.3.1917* torpedoed and sunk 5 miles S.W. of Newhaven by the German submarine UB.39 whilst on a voyage from Chittagong to the River Clyde via London with a cargo of coir matting.

71. CLAN MACGREGOR (2) (1902)
O.N. 114013. 4511 g. 2796 n. 395.7x48.2x27.0 ft.
T.3-cyl. by Greenock Foundry Co., Greenock, 398nhp.
14.12.1901 launched and *2.1902* completed by A. McMillan and Son Ltd., Dumbarton (Yard No.381) for The Clan Line Steamers Ltd. *1.6.1902* wrecked on Atlas Reef, Martha's Point, Cape Colony, whilst on a voyage from Port Natal to New York.

72. CLAN GRANT (2) (1902–1914)
O.N. 115683. 3948 g. 2505 n. 360.4x48.1x24.5 ft. Turret Deck Steamer
T.3-cyl. by the shipbuilder, 330nhp.
12.4.1902 launched and *5.1902* completed by W. Doxford and Sons Ltd., Sunderland (Yard No.296) for The Clan Line Steamers Ltd. *16.10.1914* captured by the German cruiser EMDEN and sunk by gunfire 150 miles S.W. of Minicoy, Maldive Islands, whilst on a voyage from Liverpool to Calcutta with general cargo.

73. CLAN SHAW (2) (1902–1917)
O.N. 115691. 3943 g. 2503 n. 360.0x48.1x24.5 ft. Turret Deck Steamer
T.3-cyl. by the shipbuilder, 330nhp.
10.5.1902 launched and *6.1902* completed by W. Doxford and Sons Ltd., Sunderland (Yard No.297) for The Clan Line Steamers Ltd. *23.1.1917* mined 8 miles N.E. of St. Andrews whilst on a voyage from Calcutta to Dundee with a cargo of jute. Two members of the crew lost their lives. Subsequently beached at the mouth of the River Tay and became a total loss.

74. CLAN LESLIE (1902–1916)
O.N. 115697. 3937 g. 2499 n. 359.8x48.1x24.5 ft. Turret Deck Steamer
T.3-cyl. by the shipbuilder, 330nhp.
20.6.1902 launched and *7.1902* completed by W. Doxford and Sons Ltd., Sunderland (Yard No.298) for The Clan Line Steamers Ltd. *4.11.1916* torpedoed and sunk 200 miles E. 1/2 S. from Malta by the German submarine UB.43 whilst on a voyage from Bombay to London with general cargo. Three members of the crew were lost.

75. CLAN LINDSAY (2) (1902–1931)
O.N. 115704. 3935 g. 2499 n. 360.2x48.1x24.5 ft. Turret Deck Steamer
T.3-cyl. by the shipbuilder, 330nhp.
25.7.1902 launched and *9.1902* completed by W. Doxford and Sons Ltd., Sunderland (Yard No.299) for The Clan Line Steamers Ltd. *3.5.1916* attacked by gunfire from a submarine in the Bay of Biscay and escaped. *1931* sold to T.W. Ward Ltd. and broken up at Inverkeithing.

76. CLAN CHATTAN (1) (1902–1930)
O.N. 115711. 3938 g. 2500 n. 359.8x48.1x24.4 ft. Turret Deck Steamer
T.3-cyl. by the shipbuilder, 330nhp.
3.9.1902 launched and *10.1902* completed by W. Doxford and Sons Ltd., Sunderland (Yard No.300) for The Clan Line Steamers Ltd. *1930* sold to P. & W. MacLellan Ltd. and broken up at Bo'ness.

77. CLAN MACKINNON (2) (1903–1927)
O.N. 115746. 4783 g. 3049 n. 395.4x50.9x27.0 ft.
T.3-cyl. by Denny and Co., Dumbarton, 447nhp.
30.12.1902 launched and *3.1903* completed by Wm. Denny and Bros., Dumbarton (Yard No.675) for The Clan Line Steamers Ltd. *1927* sold to Aktieb. Oceanfart (Lars Krogius manager) Finland, and renamed HERAKLES. *1936* sold for £11,000 to Stephens, Sutton Ltd., Newcastle. *1936* sold to P. & W. MacLellan Ltd. and broken up at Bo'ness under the Scrap and Build scheme.

78. CLAN MACALISTER (2) (1903–1915)
O.N. 115756. 4835 g. 3065 n. 395.0x51.1x27.0 ft.
T.3-cyl. by Dunsmuir and Jackson, Glasgow, 450nhp.
18.3.1903 launched and *4.1903* completed by A. McMillan and Son Ltd., Dumbarton (Yard No.389) for The Clan Line Steamers Ltd. *6.11.1915* captured 120 miles S. by E. from Cape Martello, Crete, by the German submarine U35 and sunk by a torpedo. She was on a voyage from Liverpool to Calcutta with general cargo.

79. CLAN MACINTYRE (2) (1903–1929)
O.N. 115775. 4807 g. 3053 n. 395.5x51.1x27.0 ft.
T.3-cyl. by Richardsons, Westgarth and Co. Ltd., Hartlepool, 452nhp.
1.4.1903 launched and *7.1903* completed by Furness, Withy and Co. Ltd., West Hartlepool (Yard No.266) for The Clan Line Steamers Ltd. *1929* sold to Soc. Anon. di Nav. Marco U. Martinolich, Italy, for £16,500 and renamed NORMA. *1932* sold to Italian shipbreakers.

80. CLAN FORBES (2) (1903–1918)
O.N. 115762. 3946 g. 2509 n. 360.3x48.1x24.5 ft. Turret Deck Steamer.
T.3-cyl. by the shipbuilder, 330nhp.
25.4.1903 launched and *6.1903* completed by W. Doxford and Sons Ltd., Sunderland (Yard No.306) for The Clan Line Steamers Ltd. *9.6.1918* torpedoed and sunk 115 miles W.N.W. of Alexandria by the German submarine UB.105 whilst on a voyage from Newport, Mon. to Port Said with a cargo of coal. Two members of the crew were lost.

81. CLAN MACNEIL (2) (1903–1918)
O.N. 115770. 3939 g. 2504 n. 360.1x48.1x24.5 ft. Turret Deck Steamer
T.3-cyl. by the shipbuilder, 330nhp.
13.5.1903 launched and *7.1903* completed by W. Doxford and Sons Ltd., Sunderland (Yard No.307) for The Clan Line Steamers Ltd. *9.11.1917* attacked by a submarine West of Gibraltar and escaped when the torpedo missed. *6.8.1918* torpedoed and sunk 10 miles North of Alexandria by the German submarine UC.34 whilst on a voyage from Karachi to Marseilles with a cargo of grain and onions.

82. CLAN MACLEOD (3) (1903–1915)
O.N. 115783. 5125 g. 3053 n. 395.5x51.1x27.0 ft.
T.3-cyl. by Richardsons, Westgarth and Co. Ltd., Hartlepool, 452nhp.
10.6.1903 launched and *10.1903* completed by Furness, Withy and Co. Ltd., West Hartlepool (Yard No.267) for The Clan Line Steamers Ltd. *1.12.1915* captured by the German submarine U33 and sunk by gunfire 100 miles E.S.E. of Malta whilst on a voyage from Chittagong to London with general cargo. Twelve members of the crew were lost.

83. CLAN MACDOUGALL (1) (1904–1918)
O.N. 119184. 4710 g. 2976 n. 385.2x50.1x26.3 ft. Turret Deck Steamer
T.3-cyl. by the shipbuilder, 413nhp.
12.10.1904 launched and *12.1904* completed by W. Doxford and Sons Ltd., Sunderland (Yard No.325) for The Clan Line Steamers Ltd. *15.3.1918* attacked by the German submarine UB.49 and sunk by torpedo and gunfire 60 miles S.E. by E. $^1/_2$ E. from Cape Carbonara, Sardinia, whilst on a voyage from Naples to Bizerta in ballast. The master and 32 crew members were lost.

84. CLAN MACNAB (2) (1905–1918)
O.N. 119199. 4675 g. 2952 n. 385.1x50.0x26.3 ft. Turret Deck Steamer.
T.3-cyl. by the shipbuilder, 413nhp.
22.11.1904 launched and *1.1905* completed by W. Doxford and Sons Ltd., Sunderland (Yard No.327) for The Clan Line Steamers Ltd. *10.5.1917* attacked by a submarine in the Mediterranean Sea and escaped when the torpedo missed. *4.8.1918* torpedoed and sunk 14 miles N.N.W. of Pendeen Lighthouse by the German submarine U113 whilst on a voyage from Plymouth to Glasgow in ballast. Twenty two crew members were lost and the survivors were rescued by the Belgian tanker steamer KASBEK, 2716/88.

85. CLAN MACLEAN (2) (1905–1919)
O.N. 121211. 4676 g. 2952 n. 385.2x50.1x26.3 ft. Turret Deck Steamer
T.3-cyl. by the shipbuilder, 413nhp.
23.1.1905 launched and *3.1905* completed by W. Doxford and Sons Ltd., Sunderland (Yard No.329) for The Clan Line Steamers Ltd. *23.11.1919* struck a rock and sank 2 miles off Mafamede Island in the Mozambique Channel whilst on a voyage from Liverpool via Delagoa Bay to Kilindini with coal and general cargo.

86. CLAN MACPHERSON (2) (1905–1918)
O.N. 121274. 4779 g. 3041 n. 400.0x51.0x27.2 ft.
T.3-cyl. by Richardsons, Westgarth and Co. Ltd., Hartlepool, 448nhp.
1.9.1905 launched and *11.1905* completed by Furness, Withy and Co. Ltd., West Hartlepool (Yard No.287) for The Clan Line Steamers Ltd. *4.3.1918* torpedoed and sunk 24 miles North of Cape Serrat by the German submarine UC.27 having sailed from Bizerta earlier in the day on a voyage from Malta to Colon. Two members of the crew were lost and a further eighteen were killed when the foremast collapsed onto a lifeboat as it prepared to leave the ship.

87. CLAN MACINTOSH (2) (1906–1932)
O.N. 121290. 4774 g. 3043 n. 400.0x51.0x27.2 ft.
T.3-cyl. by Richardsons, Westgarth and Co. Ltd., Hartlepool, 448nhp.
13.10.1905 launched and *1.1906* completed by Furness, Withy and Co. Ltd., West Hartlepool (Yard No.288) for The Clan Line Steamers Ltd. *1932* sold to Smith and Houston Ltd. and broken up at Port Glasgow.

88. CLAN MATHESON (2) (1906–1914)
O.N. 121305. 4775 g. 3053 n. 400.0x51.0x27.2 ft.
T.3-cyl. by Richardsons, Westgarth and Co. Ltd., Hartlepool, 448nhp.
27.11.1905 launched and *3.1906* completed by Furness, Withy and Co. Ltd., West Hartlepool (Yard No.289) for The Clan Line Steamers Ltd. *14.9.1914* captured by the German cruiser EMDEN and sunk by bombs 60 miles S.W. by S. from the Pilot's light at the mouth of the River Hooghly whilst on a voyage from Glasgow and Liverpool to Calcutta with general cargo.

89. CLAN GRAHAM (2) (1907–1918) and (1920)
O.N. 124211. 5213 g. 3289 n. 400.2x52.1x27.5 ft. Turret Deck Steamer
T.3-cyl. by the shipbuilder, 402nhp.
24.7.1907 launched and *9.1907* completed by W. Doxford and Sons Ltd., Sunderland (Yard No.331) for The Clan Line steamers Ltd. *26.5.1917* attacked by gunfire from a submarine in the Mediterranean Sea and escaped. *4.3.1918* torpedoed and damaged by a German submarine 15 miles S.S.E. from Cape Sidero, Crete, whilst on a voyage from Avonmouth to Port Said in ballast. Three members of the crew were lost in the attack and the ship was towed to Suda Bay. Taken over by The Shipping Controller (Sir Ernest W. Glover manager). *1920* returned to The Clan Line Steamers Ltd. *13.11.1920* badly damaged by fire whilst beached on Rammeken Bank following a collision in Flushing Roads when on a voyage from Chittagong to London and Antwerp. Abandoned as a total loss and in *1923* sold to Produits Metallurgigues Soc. Anon. and broken up in Belgium.

90. CLAN SINCLAIR (2) (1907–1933)
O.N. 124222. 5215 g. 3291 n. 400.1x52.1x27.5 ft. Turret Deck Steamer.
T.3-cyl. by the shipbuilder, 413nhp.
27.8.1907 launched and *10.1907* completed by W. Doxford and Sons Ltd., Sunderland (Yard No.333) for The Clan Line Steamers Ltd. *18.4.1917* attacked by a submarine in the North Atlantic Ocean and escaped when the torpedo missed. *1933* sold to Hughes Bolckow Shipbreaking Co. Ltd. and broken up at Blyth.

91. CLAN BUCHANAN (2) (1907–1933)
O.N. 124232. 5212 g. 3288 n. 400.1x52.1x27.4 ft. Turret Deck Steamer
T.3-cyl. by the shipbuilder, 413nhp.
24.9.1907 launched and *11.1907* completed by W. Doxford and Sons Ltd., Sunderland (Yard No.335) for The Clan Line Steamers Ltd. *12.11.1916* attacked by gunfire from a submarine off Cape Ortegal and escaped. *1933* sold to Hughes Bolckow Shipbreaking Co. Ltd. and broken up at Blyth.

92. CLAN MACINNES (1) (1907–1914)
O.N. 124329. 3755 g. 2442 n. 368.4x49.0x25.9 ft.
T.3-cyl. by Richardsons, Westgarth and Co. Ltd., Hartlepool, 320nhp.
28.12.1906 launched and *1907* completed by Furness, Withy and Co. Ltd., West Hartlepool (Yard No.299) as ROANOKE for Chesapeake & Ohio Steamship Co. Ltd. (Furness, Withy and Co. Ltd., managers), London. *1907* purchased by The Clan Line Steamers Ltd. and renamed CLAN MACINNES. *1914* sold to Furness, Withy and Co. Ltd., West Hartlepool and renamed ROANOKE. *11.2.1917* torpedoed and damaged 4 miles S.E. of Girdleness whilst on a voyage from Dundee to New York with general cargo. Towed to Dundee and subsequently repaired. *12.8.1917* captured by the German submarine UB.48 and sunk by bombs 100 miles W.N.W. of Butt of Lewis whilst on a voyage from Leith to Philadelphia with general cargo.

93. CLAN MACIVER (1) (1907–1914)
O.N. 124334. 3760 g. 2418 n. 368.4x49.0x25.9 ft.
T.3-cyl. by Richardsons, Westgarth and Co. Ltd., Hartlepool, 320nhp.
20.2.1907 launched and *1907* completed by Furness, Withy and Co. Ltd., West Hartlepool (Yard No.300) as RAPIDAN for Chesapeake & Ohio Steamship Co. Ltd. (Furness, Withy and Co. Ltd., managers), London. *1907* purchased by The Clan Line Steamers Ltd. and renamed CLAN MACIVER. *1914* sold to Furness, Withy and Co. Ltd., West Hartlepool, and renamed RAPIDAN. *1924* sold to Charles G. Dunn Shipping Co. Ltd., Liverpool, and renamed DOVENBY HALL. *1927* sold to P.M. Hadoulis & Partners, Greece, and renamed PANAGHIS M. HADOULIS. *21.1.1933* sold to Messrs Olivier & Co., Panama, and renamed MIREILLE. *1934* sold to Italian shipbreakers and broken up at Genoa.

94. CLAN MACPHEE (1911–1940)
O.N. 129578. 5165 g. 3247 n. 430.0x53.5x26.4 ft.
T.3-cyl. by Richardsons, Westgarth & Co. Ltd., Hartlepool, 497nhp.
13.6.1911 completed trials by Irvine's Shipbuilding and Dry Dock Co. Ltd., West Hartlepool (Yard No.499) for The Clan Line Steamers Ltd. *16.8.1940* torpedoed and sunk by submarine U30 in position 57° 30'N 17° 14'W, 350 miles west of North Uist on a voyage from Liverpool to East Africa and Bombay with general cargo.

95. CLAN MACKENZIE (2) (1911–1912)
O.N. 129584. 5018 g. 3134 n. 430.0x53.6x26.6 ft.
T.3-cyl by the shipbuilder, 496nhp.
8.6.1911 launched and *7.1911* completed by W. Doxford and Sons Ltd., Sunderland (Yard No.421) for The Clan Line Steamers Ltd. *30.12.1912* wrecked at Torre Nueva, near Cadiz, whilst on a voyage from the River Clyde and Newport to Colombo and Calcutta with general cargo.

96. CLAN MACGILLIVRAY (1) (1911–1948)
O.N. 129596. 5023 g. 3107 n. 430.6x53.6x26.6 ft.
T.3-cyl. by Wallsend Slipway & Engineering Co. Ltd., Wallsend, 496nhp.
12.6.1911 launched and *1911* completed by Sir W.G. Armstrong, Whitworth & Co. Ltd., Newcastle (Yard No.834) for The Clan Line Steamers Ltd. *1948* sold to Eastern Asia Navigation Co. Ltd., Hong Kong, and renamed MACLOCK. *16.1.1949* arrived Bruges to be broken up by Van Heyghen Freres. *3.2.1949* demolition commenced.

97. CLAN MACNAUGHTON (1) (1911–1915)
O.N. 129592. 4985 g. 3103 n. 429.8x53.7x34.6 ft.
T.3-cyl. by the shipbuilder, 496nhp.
28.6.1911 launched and *8.1911* completed by A. Stephen and Sons Ltd., Glasgow (Yard No.443) for The Clan Line Steamers Ltd. *19.11.1914* hired for service as an Armed Merchant Cruiser (Pennant No.M.81), armed with eight 4.7" guns and attached to the 10th Cruiser Squadron. *3.2.1915* last heard from whilst on patrol off the North coast of Ireland. Presumed to have foundered with the loss of 20 officers and 261 ratings.

98. CLAN MACRAE (3) (1912–1921)
O.N. 133005. 5058 g. 3166 n.430.0x53.5x26.6 ft.
T.3-cyl. by shipbuilder, 496nhp.
21.11.1911 launched and *1.1912* completed by W. Doxford and Sons Ltd., Sunderland (Yard No.429) for The Clan Line Steamers Ltd. *9.1914* aided crew of H.M.S. PEGASUS after she was sunk at Zanzibar by German cruiser KÖNIGSBERG. *10.1914* towed H.M.S. CHATHAM off Leven Rocks near Kilindini, Mombasa. *9.3.1915* chased by a submarine off Liverpool Bar Light Vessel, managed to escape. *1921* transferred to the British and South American Steam Navigation Co. Ltd. (Houston Line, managers) and renamed BANFFSHIRE. *29.9.1943* torpedoed and sunk by submarine U532 in position 9° 26'N 71° 20'E, 380 miles S.W. from Mangalore.

99. CLAN DAVIDSON (1) (1912–1917)
O.N. 133017. 5058 g. 3166 n. 430.0x53.5x26.6 ft.
T.3-cyl. by shipbuilder, 496nhp.
19.12.1911 launched and *2.1912* completed by W. Doxford and Sons Ltd., Sunderland (Yard No.431) for The Clan Line Steamers Ltd. *24.6.1917* torpedoed and sunk by submarine UC.17 130 miles S.W. by W $1/4$ W from the Scillies while on a voyage from Brisbane to London with general cargo.

100. CLAN MACEWEN (1912–1920)
O.N. 133053. 5140 g. 3190 n. 430.5x53.6x26.6 ft.
T.3-cyl. by shipbuilder, 496nhp.
16.3.1912 launched and *1912* completed by Palmers Shipbuilding & Iron Co. Ltd., Jarrow (Yard No.817) for The Clan Line Steamers Ltd. *1920* transferred to the British and South American Steam Navigation Co. Ltd. (Houston Line, managers) and renamed BUTESHIRE. *25.2.1948* arrived at Preston for scrapping.

101. CLAN MACARTHUR (2) (1912–1921)
O.N. 133085. 5815 g. 3614 n. 450.1x57.1x26.8 ft.
T.3-cyl. by Wallsend Slipway and Engineering Co. Ltd., Wallsend, 574nhp.
26.9.1912 launched and *1912* completed by Sir W.G. Armstrong, Whitworth and Co. Ltd., Newcastle (Yard No.846) for The Clan Line Steamers Ltd. *27.4.1917* chased by a submarine off Scilly Isles but managed to escape. *1912* transferred to Scottish Shire Line (Turnbull, Martin and Co., managers) and renamed BERWICKSHIRE. *20.8.1944* torpedoed and sunk by submarine U861 in position 30° 58'S 38° 50'E, 500 miles E.S.E. of Durban while on a voyage from Durban to Tamatave and Mauritius.

102. CLAN MACBRIDE (1) (1912–1937)
O.N. 133087. 4922 g. 3009 n. 390.0x50.5x27.9 ft.
T.3-cyl. by Blair and Co., Stockton, 393nhp.
19.12.1912 completed trials by Ropner and Sons Ltd., Stockton (Yard No.474) for The Clan Line Steamers Ltd. *1937* sold to McCowen and Gross Ltd., London, under the Scrap and Build Scheme and renamed HEATHCOT. *1938* broken up.

103. CLAN MACKELLAR (1) (1913–1937)
O.N. 133105. 6382 g. 4682 n. 410.2x52.0x27.9 ft.
T.3-cyl. by Earles Co. Ltd., Hull, 601nhp.
7.12.1912 launched as HARFLETE for J. & C. Harrison Ltd., London, and *3.1913* completed as CLAN MACKELLAR for The Clan Line Steamers Ltd. by Northumberland Shipbuilding Co. Ltd., Willington-on-Tyne (Yard No.208). *1937* sold to McCowen and Gross Ltd., London, under the Scrap and Build Scheme and renamed MOORCOT. *1939* broken up.

104. CLAN MACTAVISH (1) (1913–1916)
O.N. 133100. 5816 g. 3626 n. 450.1x57.1x26.8 ft.
T.3-cyl. by Wallsend Slipway and Engineering Co. Ltd., Wallsend, 574nhp.
9.12.1912 launched and *1913* completed by Sir W.G. Armstrong, Whitworth & Co. Ltd., Newcastle (Yard No.847) for The Clan Line Steamers Ltd. *16.1.1916* sunk by German raider MOEWE in position 30° 40'N 17° 10'W, 120 miles S.W. of Funchal on a voyage from Wellington to London with general cargo, eighteen Indian crew killed, three taken prisoner.

105. CLAN MACBETH (1) (1913–1938)
O.N. 133120. 4647 g. 2950 n. 385.0x51.7x27.4 ft.
T.3-cyl. by Richardsons, Westgarth & Co. Ltd., Hartlepool, 394nhp.
19.2.1913 launched and *5.1913* completed by Sir James Laing & Sons Ltd., Sunderland (Yard No.640) for The Clan Line Steamers Ltd. *1937* sold to Nailsea Steamship Co. Ltd. (E.R. Management Co. Ltd.) for £16.250 and renamed NAILSEA VALE. *1938* broken up under the Scrap and Build Scheme.

106. CLAN MACCORQUODALE (1913–1917)
O.N. 133153. 5121 g. 3180 n. 430.2x53.4x26.7 ft.
T.3-cyl. by Dunsmuir & Jackson, Glasgow, 679nhp.
4.9.1913 launched and *11.1913* completed by C. Connell & Co. Ltd., Glasgow (Yard No.354) for The Clan Line Steamers Ltd. *17.11.1917* torpedoed and sunk by submarine UB.51 165 miles N.N.W. from Alexandria while on a voyage from Madras to London with general cargo.

107. CLAN MACQUARRIE (1) (1913–1942)
O.N. 133157. 5060 g. 3152 n. 429.2x53.7x26.6 ft.
T.3-cyl. by shipbuilder, 496nhp.
16.9.1913 launched and *11.1913* completed by A. Stephens and Sons Ltd., Glasgow (Yard No.456) for The Clan Line Steamers Ltd. *1914* requisitioned by the Admiralty as a Royal Naval Squadron supply ship. *13.6.1942* sunk by torpedo and gunfire from Italian submarine DA VINCI in position 5° 30'N 23° 30'W, 600 miles from Freetown.

108. CLAN CAMPBELL (3) (1914–1916)
O.N. 136320. 5897 g. 3680 n. 430.2x54.3x29.4 ft.
T.3-cyl by Dunsmuir & Jackson, Glasgow, 413nhp.
6.8.1914 launched and *12.1914* completed by Napier & Miller Ltd., Glasgow (Yard No.196) for The Clan Line Steamers Ltd. *3.4.1916* torpedoed and sunk by submarine U39 29 miles S.E. of Cape Bon on a voyage from Tuticorin to London with general cargo.

109. CLAN ROSS (2) (1914–1942)
O.N. 136330. 5897 g. 3757 n. 430.0x54.3x29.4 ft.
T.3-cyl. by shipbuilder, 413nhp.
4.9.1914 launched and *11.1914* completed by Swan, Hunter & Wigham Richardson Ltd., Wallsend (Yard No.959) for The Clan Line Steamers Ltd. *5.5.1918* torpedoed by submarine 28 miles East of Cape Camerat, arrived Toulon safely, while on a voyage from Naples and Genoa to Buenos Aires in ballast, nine lives lost. *24.6.1940* attacked and damaged by aircraft in position 46° 17'N 40° 35'W while homeward bound from India, reached Milford Haven safely. *2.4.1942* torpedoed and sunk by Japanese submarine I–6 in position 15° 58'N 68° 24'E, 450 miles S.W. from Bombay.

110. CLAN OGILVY (2) (1914–1941)
O.N. 137782. 5802 g. 3716 n. 430.0x54.2x29.4 ft.
T.3-cyl. by shipbuilder, 413nhp.
20.10.1914 launched and *12.1914* completed by W. Doxford and Sons Ltd., Sunderland (Yard No.470) for The Clan Line Steamers Ltd. *30.6.1940* damaged by E-boat off St. Catherine's Point, Isle of Wight, but reached Falmouth safely. *20.3.1941* torpedoed and sunk by submarine U105 in position 20° 4'N 25° 45'W, 550 miles N.W. of Dakar in homeward convoy S.L.68 from Freetown which had sailed *12.3.1941*.

111. CLAN MACBRAYNE (1) (1916–1948)
O.N. 137811. 4818 g. 2978 n. 390.0x50.5x28.0 ft.
T.3-cyl. by Blair & Co., Stockton, 403nhp.
3.2.1916 launched and *4.1916* completed by Ropner and Sons Ltd., Stockton (Yard No.504) for The Clan Line Steamers Ltd. *1948* sold to C. Galanos Steamship Co., Panama, and renamed SAN GEORGIO. *24.10.1950* arrived Barrow to be broken up by T.W. Ward Ltd.

112. CLAN STUART (3) (1916–1940)
O.N. 137827. 5760 g. 3382 n. 423.5x56.0x28.7 ft.
T.3-cyl. by J.G. Kincaid & Co. Ltd., Greenock, 538nhp.
1930 fitted with a Bauer-Wach LP exhaust turbine, 627nhp.
29.7.1916 launched and *10.1916* completed by Russell & Co., Port Glasgow (Yard No.689) for The Clan Line Steamers Ltd. *22.12.1916* missed by torpedo from a submarine in the Mediterranean. *11.3.1940* sunk by collision in the English Channel off Start Point.

113. CLAN MACKAY (3) (1917–1918)
O.N. 137829. 6580 g. 4190 n. 420.0x53.4x36.3 ft.
T.3-cyl. by N.E. Marine Engineering Co. Ltd., Newcastle, 662nhp.
17.7.1916 launched and *1.1917* completed by Northumberland Shipbuilding Co. Ltd., Willington-on-Tyne (Yard No.229) for The Clan Line Steamers Ltd. *11.5.1918* sank following a collision with the British steamer EURYPYLUS 5691/12, 520 miles S.W. of Scilly Isles while on a voyage from Liverpool to Calcutta with general cargo.

114. CLAN MATHESON (3) (1917–1918)
O.N. 137858. 5960 g. 3736 n. 405.0x53.5x33.5 ft.
T.3-cyl. by G. Clark Ltd., Sunderland, 401nhp.
14.7.1916 launched and *1.1917* completed by Sir James Laing & Sons Ltd., Sunderland, for The Clan Line Steamers Ltd. *23.5.1918* sunk in collision with the American steamer WESTERN COAST 5730/18 in position 40° 32'N 49° 10'W while on a voyage from New Orleans and New York to Nantes with a cargo of barley, oats and steel.

115. CLAN RANALD (3) (1917–1947)
O.N. 137833. 5447 g. 3446 n. 409.1x54.0x28.9 ft.
T.3-cyl. by J.G. Kincaid & Co.Ltd., Greenock, 538nhp.
3.1917 completed by Napier & Miller Ltd., Glasgow (Yard No.199) for The Clan Line Steamers Ltd. *27.2.1933* in collision with the French steamer PSYCHE in Oran Harbour. *1947* sold to Pace Brothers Ltd., Malta, and renamed VALETTA CITY. *1951* sold to Soc. di Nav. Vecchia Genova, Genoa (Pala & Franceschini, managers) and renamed LA VALETTA. *25.3.1958* laid-up at La Spezia and *7.1958* demolition commenced there.

116. CLAN MALCOLM (1) (1917–1935)
O.N. 137837. 5994 g. 3724 n. 405.1x53.3x33.5 ft.
T.3-cyl. by Blair & Co., Stockton, 402nhp.
9.11.1916 launched and *1917* completed by Craig, Taylor & Co., Stockton (Yard No.172) for The Clan Line Steamers Ltd. *6.1921* collided with ferry ROWAN off Corsewall Point near Stranraer. *26.9.1935* wrecked on Tregwin Rocks, Green Lane Cove, Lizard, while on a voyage from Port Natal to Glasgow via London with a cargo of maize. Struck rocks at 2000 hours.

117. CLAN MACKENZIE (3) (1917–1938)
O.N. 137849. 6500 g. 4160 n. 420.1x53.4x36.3 ft.
T.3-cyl. by N.E. Marine Engineering Co. Ltd., Newcastle, 610nhp.
1930 fitted with a Bauer-Wach LP exhaust turbine, 698nhp.
6.1917 completed by Northumberland Shipbuilding Co. Ltd., Willington-on-Tyne (Yard No.231) for The Clan Line Steamers Ltd. *5.3.1918* torpedoed by submarine off St. Catherine's Point on a voyage from Liverpool to Plymouth with chalk, reached Southampton safely, six lives lost. *4.1933* damaged by a fire in No.2 hold, beached at Syracuse to extinguish flames. *23.10.1937* beached in Liverpool Bay after colliding with MANCHESTER REGIMENT 7930/22 when leaving Liverpool for East London. *3.1938* refloated at a cost of £10,000 and broken up by West of Scotland Shipbreaking Co. Ltd. at Troon. Subsequent enquiry apportioned blame as 80% to MANCHESTER REGIMENT and 20% to CLAN MACKENZIE.

118. CLAN MACMASTER (1917–1923)
O.N. 140696. 6563 g. 4137 n. 420.0x54.0x34.4 ft.
T.3-cyl. by Richardsons, Westgarth & Co. Ltd., Hartlepool, 568nhp.
24.2.1917 launched for B.J. Sutherland & Co. Ltd., Newcastle, as SUTHERLAND by W. Doxford & Sons Ltd., Sunderland (Yard No.481) and *8.1917* completed for The Clan Line Steamers Ltd. as CLAN MACMASTER. *30.9.1923* wrecked on Thousla Rock, Calf of Man, while on a voyage from the Clyde to Liverpool.

119. CLAN KEITH (1) (1918–1920) and (1924–1937)
O.N. 136654. 4306 g. 2685 n. 385.0x52.0x25.1 ft.
T.3-cyl. by J. Dickinson & Sons Ltd., Sunderland, 401nhp.
13.1.1914 launched and *3.1914* completed by Bartram & Sons Ltd., Sunderland (Yard No.231) as ETONIAN for Cambrian Steam Navigation Co. Ltd. (J. Mathias, manager), Cardiff. *1918* purchased by The Clan Line Steamers Ltd. *1920* transferred to the British and South American Steam Navigation Co. Ltd. (Houston Line, managers) and renamed HILARIUS. *1924* transferred back to The Clan Line Steamers Ltd. *1937* sold to Minster Steamship Co. Ltd., London, for £23,000 and renamed ORMINSTER. *1940* sold to South American Saint Line (B. & S. Shipping Co. Ltd.). *23.8.1944* torpedoed and sunk by submarine U480 in position 50° 09'N 0° 44'W, 35 miles N.W. of Cap d'Antifer while returning from the Normandy beaches, six crew lost.

120. CLAN MACBEAN (1) (1918–1947)
O.N. 141876. 5052 g. 3082 n. 400.0x52.4x28.0 ft.
T.3-cyl. by J. Dickinson & Sons Ltd., Sunderland, 476nhp.
31.10.1917 launched by Bartram & Sons Ltd., Sunderland (Yard No.243) for G. Swainton & Co., Newcastle, and *1.1918* completed for The Clan Line Steamers Ltd. *18.10.1939* missed by torpedo from submarine in position 45°N 15°W approx. on a voyage from India to Liverpool via Gibraltar. *1947* sold to Okeanis Shipping Co. Ltd. (Goulandris Brothers, managers) and renamed KORTHION. *1950* sold to Ubaldo Gennari Fu Torquato, Rimini and renamed AUDAX. *8.6.1959* arrived Yawata, Japan, for scrapping.

121. CLAN MORRISON (1918–1940)
O.N. 141877. 5931 g. 3698 n. 409.6x53.5x33.5 ft.
T.3-cyl. by Dunsmuir & Jackson, Glasgow, 413nhp.
19.12.1917 completed trials by Ayrshire Dockyard Co. Ltd., Irvine (Yard No.457) for The Clan Line Steamers Ltd. *24.2.1940* mined and sunk in North Sea off Cromer in position 53° 07'N 1° 22'E while on a voyage from Southampton to Blyth in ballast.

122. CLAN MACVICAR (1918–1936)
O.N. 141878. 5815 g. 3621 n. 400.1x53.0x32.8 ft.
T.3-cyl. by N.E. Marine Engineering Co. Ltd., Newcastle, 569nhp.
15.12.1917 launched as MAENWEN for W. & C.T. Jones Steamship Co. Ltd., Cardiff, and *3.1918* completed for The Clan Line Steamers Ltd. as CLAN MACVICAR. *1936* sold to Dover Hill Steamship Co. Ltd. (Counties Ship Management Co. Ltd.), London, and renamed DOVER HILL. *2.1944* taken over by Ministry of War Transport, J. & J. Denholm appointed managers. *4.4.1943* damaged by bombing at Mishukov Anchorage, Kola Inlet. *9.6.1944* sunk as a blockship at Normandy.

123. CLAN ALPINE (3) (1918–1943)
O.N. 141879. 5442 g. 3390 n. 410.2x53.5x28.4 ft.
T.3-cyl. by J.G. Kincaid & Co. Ltd., Greenock, 538nhp.
1930 fitted with a Bauer-Wach LP exhaust turbine, 627nhp.
28.1.1918 launched and *4.1918* completed by Greenock and Grangemouth Dockyard Co. Ltd., Greenock (Yard No.379) for The Clan Line Steamers Ltd. *13.3.1943* torpedoed by U107 in position 42° 45'N 13° 31'W, 190 miles west of Finisterre on a voyage from Liverpool to Gibraltar, and sunk by an escort in convoy OS44.

124. CLAN MONROE (3) (1918–1940)
O.N. 141882. 5913 g. 3699 n. 409.6x53.4x33.5 ft.
T.3-cyl. by Dunsmuir & Jackson, Glasgow, 413nhp.
3.4.1918 completed trials by Ayrshire Dockyard Co. Ltd., Irvine (Yard No.466) for The Clan Line Steamers Ltd. *2.1924* aground in the Suez Canal, refloated after lightening. *29.7.1940* mined and sunk 25 miles East of Harwich in position 51° 52'N 1° 48'E, having just sailed from Southend.

125. CLAN MACMILLAN (2) (1918–1924)
O.N. 141883. 6560 g. 4120 n. 420.0x54.0x34.4 ft.
T.3-cyl. by Richardsons, Westgarth & Co. Ltd., Hartlepool, 567nhp.
29.12.1917 launched by W. Doxford & Sons Ltd., Sunderland (Yard No.517) as DUMFRIES for B.J. Sutherland & Co. Ltd., Newcastle, and *3.1918* completed as CLAN MACMILLAN for The Clan Line Steamers Ltd. *20.6.1924* wrecked on Preparis Island, Bay of Bengal, after striking a reef on a voyage from Calcutta to Nukualofa, Tonga, with general cargo.

126. CLAN MACVEY (1918)
O.N. 141884. 5830 g. 3710 n. 400.0x53.0x32.8 ft.
T.3-cyl. by N.E. Marine Engineering Co. Ltd., Newcastle, 569nhp.
25.4.1918 launched and *7.1918* completed by Northumberland Shipbuilding Co. Ltd., Willington-on-Tyne (Yard No.245) for The Clan Line Steamers Ltd. *7.8.1918* missed by torpedo from submarine, but on the following day torpedoed by UB.57 ½ mile SE of Anvil Point and sank 5 miles NW of the Needles. She was on her maiden voyage from Newcastle to Port Said with coal.

127. CLAN MACBEOLAN (1918–1920)
O.N. 131427. 4652 g. 2903 n. 385.0x51.5x27.4 ft.
T.3-cyl. by Blair & Co., Stockton, 419nhp.
2.2.1912 launched and *3.1912* completed by Craig, Taylor & Co., Stockton (Yard No.149) as LORD CROMER for SS Lord Lathom Co. Ltd. (J. Herron & Co., managers), Liverpool. *1918* purchased by The Clan Line Steamers Ltd. and renamed CLAN MACBEOLAN. *1920* transferred to British and South American Steam Navigation Co. Ltd. (Houston Line, managers) and renamed HALESIUS. *1936* sold to N. Sitinas & Co., Andros, and renamed AVRA. *25.9.1941* sank in collision off Duncansby Head.

128. CLAN KENNETH (1) (1918–1934)
O.N. 127551. 5100 g. 3184 n. 400.0x52.0x27.4 ft.
T.3-cyl. by Rankin & Blackmore, Glasgow, 479nhp.
17.8.1909 launched and *9.1909* completed as ARDGRYFE for SS Ardgyfe Co. (Lang & Fulton Ltd.), London. *1918* purchased by The Clan Line Steamers Ltd. and renamed CLAN KENNETH. *1934* broken up at Blyth by Hughes Bolckow & Co. Ltd.

129. CLAN KENNEDY (1) (1918–1924)
O.N. 123539. 5086 g. 3198 n. 400.0x52.0x19.3 ft.
T.3-cyl. by Rankin & Blackmore, Glasgow, 471nhp.
11.9.1907 launched and *10.1907* completed by Russell & Co., Glasgow (Yard No.570) as OTTERBURN for Burn Line (R. Shankland, manager). *1912* sold to SS Ardgarroch Co. Ltd. (Lang & Fulton Ltd.), London, and renamed ARDGARROCH. *1918* purchased by The Clan Line Steamers Ltd. and renamed CLAN KENNEDY. *16.1.1924* stranded 1 mile north of Thorpness, Suffolk, on the Sizewall Bank on a voyage from New Caledonia to Hamburg and London with ore and copra. *1.1924* refloated and sold to J. Cashmore, Newport, for breaking up.

130. CLAN MACKINLAY (1) (1918–1940)
O.N. 141890. 6365 g. 4135 n. 420.0x54.5x34.0 ft.
T.3-cyl. by D. Rowan & Co. Ltd., Glasgow, 667nhp.
1930 fitted with a Bauer-Wach LP exhaust turbine, 781nhp.
9.1918 launched and *11.1918* completed by W. Hamilton & Co. Ltd., Port Glasgow (Yard No.308) for The Clan Line Steamers Ltd. *6.11.1940* bombed and sunk by aircraft off Noss Head, Wick, in position 58° 33'N 2° 53'W, moving round fully loaded to Methil from the Clyde, where she had arrived from India via South Africa.

131. CLAN QUHELE/CLAN MACWILLIAM (1918–1927)
O.N. 141892. 6086 g. 3774 n. 423.5x55.9x28.8 ft.
T.3-cyl. by J.G. Kincaid & Co. Ltd., Greenock, 538nhp.
23.10.1918 launched as CLAN QUHELE and *12.1918* completed as CLAN MACWILLIAM by Greenock & Grangemouth Dockyard Co. Ltd. (Yard No.385) for The Clan Line Steamers Ltd. *6.1923* damaged propeller against quay wall while manoeuvring at Dunkirk. *1.1924* suffered engine trouble, put into Panama. *24.12.1927* lost by fire at Vavau, Friendly Islands, while loading copra and general cargo for U.K., master and chief engineer lost.

132. CLAN MURRAY (3) (1918–1949)
O.N. 141894. 5954 g. 3422 n. 409.5x53.5x33.5 ft.
T.3-cyl. by Dunsmuir & Jackson, Glasgow, 413nhp.
1932 fitted with a Bauer-Wach LP exhaust turbine, 513nhp.
22.10.1918 launched and *12.1918* completed by Ayrshire Dockyard Co. Ltd., Irvine (Yard No.472) for The Clan Line Steamers Ltd. *5.1942* rescued survivors of P. & O. cargoship SOUDAN mined off Cape Agulhas, South Africa. *1949* transferred to British and South American Steam Navigation Co. Ltd. (Houston Line, managers) and renamed HALIZONES. *17.6.1952* arrived Bo'ness to be scrapped by P. & W. MacLellan Ltd.

133. CLAN SKENE (1919–1920) and (1923–1942)
O.N. 141893. 5214 g. 3222 n. 401.0x52.3x28.5 ft.
T.3-cyl. by D. Rowan & Co. Ltd., Glasgow, 517nhp.
1930 fitted with a Bauer-Wach LP exhaust turbine, 599nhp.
11.1918 launched as WAR ADDER for The Shipping Controller and *1.1919* completed as CLAN SKENE by C. Connell & Co. Ltd., Glasgow (Yard No.389) for The Clan Line steamers Ltd. *1920* transferred to British and South American Steam Navigation Co. Ltd. (Houston Line, managers) and renamed HALOCRATES. *4.7.1923* stranded in the Strait of Kanso, Nova Scotia, refloated and towed to New York. *1923* transferred back to The Clan Line Steamers Ltd. *10.5.1942* torpedoed and sunk by U333 in position 31° 43'N 70° 43'W, 360 miles SE from Cape Hatteras while on a voyage from Cape Town to North America.

134. CLAN MORGAN/CLAN MATHESON (4) (1919–1948)
O.N. 141896. 5613 g. 3450 n. 397.1x51.4x34.0 ft.
T.3-cyl. by D. Rowan & Co. Ltd., Glasgow, 517nhp.
2.1919 launched as CLAN MORGAN and *4.1919* completed as CLAN MATHESON by W. Hamilton & Co. Ltd., Port Glasgow (Yard No.311) for The Clan Line Steamers Ltd. *5.12.1943* damaged by bombs at Calcutta. *1948* transferred to British and South American Steam Navigation Co. Ltd. (Houston Line, managers) and renamed HARMODIUS. *1951* sold to Heron Steamship Co. Ltd., London (Tsavliris Shipping Co., managers) and renamed CLAIRE T. *1955* sold to Ministry of Transport and renamed EMPIRE CLAIRE. *27.7.1955* left Stranraer to be scuttled off the Atlantic shelf in position 12°W 56° 30'N with war material.

135. CLAN MURDOCH (1) (1919–1948)
O.N. 141911. 5950 g. 3422 n. 409.6x53.5x33.5 ft.
T.3-cyl. by Dunsmuir & Jackson, Glasgow, 560nhp.
1930 fitted with a Bauer-Wach LP exhaust turbine, 674nhp.
15.4.1919 launched and *7.1919* completed by Ayrshire Dockyard Co. Ltd., Irvine (Yard No.473) for The Clan Line Steamers Ltd. *1948* transferred to British and South American Steam Navigation Co. Ltd. (Houston Line, managers) and renamed HALESIUS. *1952* sold to Cia Capo Bona Esperanza SA, Panama, and renamed JANKIKI. *28.11.1953* foundered off Berlengo Island, 50 miles north of Lisbon in heavy weather after her cargo of phosphate had shifted on a voyage from Casablanca to Holland.

136. CLAN MACKAY (4) (1919–1934)
O.N. 136793. 5182 g. 3205 n. 420.0x54.1x26.3 ft.
T.3-cyl. by shipbuilder, 577nhp.
3.6.1913 launched and *7.1913* completed by W. Doxford & Sons Ltd., Sunderland (Yard No.455) for Hamburg-America Line, Hamburg, as SÜDMARK. *17.8.1914* captured by Royal Navy, taken into Suez while on a voyage from Yokohama to Hamburg. *9.1914* requisitioned by The Shipping Controller, management taken over by Harris & Dixon Ltd. *1915* renamed HUNTSCRAFT. *1917* management taken over by Union-Castle Line. *1919* purchased by The Clan Line Steamers Ltd. *1921* renamed CLAN MACKAY. *19.10.1934* wrecked on Carpenters Rock, Sierra Leone, while on a voyage from Cairns, Australia to Montreal, struck reef at 0710 hours.

137. CLAN MACINNES (2) (1920–1947)
O.N. 141940. 4672 g. 2826 n. 384.8x52.0x26.7 ft.
T.3-cyl. by Rankin & Blackmore, Glasgow, 517nhp.
6.11.1919 launched and *1.1920* completed by Lithgows Ltd., Port Glasgow (Yard No.727) for The Clan Line Steamers Ltd. *5.5.1941* damaged by bombs at Liverpool. *1947* sold to Noemijulia Steamship Co. Ltd., London, and renamed SAN GEORGE. *1948* registered under Kenfig Steamship Co. Ltd., London (S. Catsell & Co. Ltd., managers). *1951* sold to Indian National Steamship Co. Ltd., Calcutta, and renamed SIVA-SHAMBHU. *1955* broken up at Calcutta.

138. CLAN MACTAGGART (1) (1920–1942)
O.N. 144223. 7603 g. 4776 n. 452.6x57.7x29.6 ft.
Two Steam Turbines by Scotts Shipbuilding & Engineering Co. Ltd., Greenock, DR geared to a single screw shaft, 905nhp.
17.6.1920 launched and *11.1920* completed by Ayrshire Dockyard Co. Ltd., Irvine (Yard No.474) for The Clan Line Steamers Ltd. *11.10.1940* damaged by bombs at Liverpool. *16.11.1942* torpedoed and sunk by U92 in position 36° 08'N 7° 23'W, 100 miles W of Gibraltar on a voyage from Gibraltar to Liverpool, having just taken part in the North African landings.

139. CLAN MACNAB (3) (1920–1941)
O.N. 144229. 6076 g. 3705 n. 410.6x53.3x33.4 ft.
T.3-cyl. by Dunsmuir & Jackson, Glasgow, 560nhp.
1930 fitted with a Bauer-Wach LP exhaust turbine, 692nhp.
12.8.1920 launched and *12.1920* completed by Ayrshire Dockyard Co. Ltd., Irvine (Yard No.485) for The Clan Line Steamers Ltd. *17.3.1941* sunk by collision east of Cape Verde Islands in a homeward convoy from Freetown which had sailed *12.3.1941.*

140. CLAN MACINDOE (1) (1920–1943)
O.N. 144233. 4635 g. 2775 n. 384.8x52.0x26.7 ft.
T.3-cyl. by Rankin & Blackmore, Glasgow, 517nhp.
1930 fitted with Bauer-Wach LP exhaust turbine, 613nhp.
11.11.1920 launched and *12.1920* completed by Lithgows Ltd., Port Glasgow (Yard No.728) for The Clan Line Steamers Ltd. *27.4.1943* lost after fire and stranding at Alexandria.

141. CLAN MACTAVISH (2) (1921–1942)
O.N. 144252. 7603 g. 4776 n. 452.6x57.7x29.6 ft.
Two Steam Turbines by Scotts Shipbuilding & Engineering Co. Ltd., Greenock, DR geared to a single screw shaft, 905nhp.
25.11.1920 launched and *5.1921* completed by Ayrshire Dockyard Co. Ltd., Irvine (Yard No.475) for The Clan Line Steamers Ltd. *8.10.1942* torpedoed and sunk by U159 in position 34° 53'S 16° 45'E, 250 miles West of Cape of Good Hope, while on a voyage from Durban to New York.

142. CLAN MACIVER (2) (1921–1951)
O.N. 144253. 4500 g. 2810 n. 384.8x52.0x26.5 ft.
T.3-cyl. by Rankin & Blackmore, Glasgow, 517nhp.

6.5.1921 launched and *6.1921* completed by Lithgows Ltd., Port Glasgow (Yard No.737) for The Clan Line Steamers Ltd. *1951* sold to Cie Maritima Carrena SA, Costa Rica, and renamed CARRENA. *1953* sold to Gulf Steamships Ltd., Pakistan, and renamed MUSTALI. *1961* sold for scrap for £72,500.

143. CLAN MACNAIR (1) (1921–1953)
O.N. 144259. 6096 g. 3820 n. 410.7x53.3x33.4 ft.
T.3-cyl. by Dunsmuir & Jackson, Glasgow, 560nhp.
1930 fitted with a Bauer-Wach LP exhaust turbine, 639nhp.
25.3.1921 launched and *10.1921* completed by Ayrshire Dockyard Co. Ltd., Irvine (Yard No.486) for The Clan Line Steamers Ltd. *15.9.1952* arrived Blyth to be scrapped by Hughes Bolckow Ltd.

144. CLAN MACNAUGHTON (2) (1921–1942)
O.N. 146259. 6110 g. 3820 n. 410.5x53.3x33.4 ft.
T.3-cyl. by Dunsmuir & Jackson, Glasgow, 561nhp.
1929 fitted with a Bauer-Wach LP exhaust turbine, 639nhp.
9.8.1921 launched and *10.1921* completed by Ayrshire Dockyard Co. Ltd., Irvine (Yard No.488) for The Clan Line Steamers Ltd. *1.8.1942* torpedoed and sunk by U155 in position 11° 54'N 54° 25'W, 480 miles east of Trinidad while on a voyage from the U.K. to Trinidad.

145. CLAN MACNEIL (3) (1922–1953)
O.N. 146281. 6111 g. 3788 n. 410.5x53.3x33.4 ft.
T.3-cyl. by Dunsmuir & Jackson, Glasgow, 560nhp.
1930 fitted with a Bauer-Wach LP exhaust turbine, 691nhp.
1.12.1921 launched and *2.1922* completed by Ayrshire Dockyard Co. Ltd., Irvine (Yard No.489) for The Clan Line Steamers Ltd. *2.5.1952* arrived Port Glasgow to be scrapped by Smith & Houston Ltd.

146. CLAN MACFARLANE (2) (1922–1940)
O.N. 146317. 6196 g. 3735 n. 418.1x53.4x33.6 ft.
T.3-cyl. by Dunsmuir & Jackson, Glasgow, 630nhp.
1930 fitted with a Bauer-Wach LP exhaust turbine, 743nhp.
24.8.1922 launched by Miss Parr and *11.1922* completed by Ayrshire Dockyard Co. Ltd., Irvine (Yard No.491) for The Clan Line steamers Ltd. *17.6.1940* sunk by collision off Socotra, half of the crew and 20 Askari soldiers were lost.

147. CLAN MACFADYEN (2) (1923–1942)
O.N. 146335. 6191 g. 3779 n. 418.2x53.4x33.6 ft.
T.3-cyl. by Dunsmuir & Jackson, Glasgow, 630nhp.
1929 fitted with a Bauer-Wach LP exhaust turbine, 743nhp.
15.2.1923 launched and *5.1923* completed by Ayrshire Dockyard Co. Ltd., Irvine (Yard No.490) for The Clan Line Steamers Ltd. *4.8.1937* in collision with H.M.S. FAULKNOR. *26.11.1942* torpedoed and sunk by U508 in position 8° 57'N 58° 48'W, 100 miles from Port of Spain, Trinidad.

148. CLAN MACWHIRTER (1923–1942)
O.N. 142598. 5941 g. 3702 n. 424.4x55.8x28.8 ft.
T.3-cyl. by J.G. Kincaid & Co. Ltd., Greenock, 549nhp.
26.4.1918 launched and *7.1918* completed by Lloyd Royal Belge (GB) Ltd., Glasgow (Yard No.3) as YPRESVILLE for Lloyd Royal Belge, Belgium. *1919* sold to British and South American Steam Navigation Co. Ltd. (Houston Line, managers) and renamed HALIZONES. *1920* sold to Convoy Steamship Co. Ltd. (H.D. Kempt. manager) and renamed WILLCASINO. *1923* purchased by The Clan Line Steamers Ltd. and renamed CLAN MACWHIRTER. *26.8.1942* torpedoed and sunk by U156 in position 35° 45'N 18° 45'W, 200 miles north of Madeira.

149. CLAN MACILWRAITH (1) (1924–1950)
O.N. 147931. 4839 g. 2878 n. 387.4x52.2x27.6 ft.
T.3-cyl. by McKie & Baxter, Glasgow, 557nhp.
14.8.1924 launched and *11.1924* completed by Greenock Dockyard Co. Ltd., Greenock (Yard No.403) for The Clan Line Steamers Ltd. *1950* sold to F.A. Vinnen, Bremen, and renamed MAGDALENE VINNEN. *1956* sold to Cia Nav. Vaptistes SA, Costa Rica, and renamed SAN GEORGE. *18.4.1958* arrived Antwerp for scrapping.

150. COLIMA (1926–1930)
O.N. 146269. 1393 g. 819 n. 255.9x35.0x15.4 ft.
T.4-cyl. by shipbuilder, 219nhp.
24.9.1917 launched and *11.1917* completed by Lobnitz & Co. Ltd., Renfrew (Yard No.826) as POLYANTHUS for the Admiralty. *1922* sold to Cia Nav. de los Estados do Mexico SA, Mexico, renamed COLIMA. *1926* purchased by The Clan Line Steamers Ltd., name unchanged. *1930* sold to British Trade Crusades, Glasgow. *1933* sold to Antoniou & Katarmados, Piraeus, and renamed ACROPOLIS. *6.4.1941* lost while at Piraeus during an air-raid.

151. NAYARIT (1926–1928)
O.N. 146296. 1461 g. 850 n. 255.2x35.0x16.2 ft.
T.4-cyl. by Richardsons, Westgarth & Co. Ltd., Hartlepool, 237nhp.
31.10.1917 launched and *4.1918* completed by Blyth Shipbuilding and Dry Dock Co. Ltd., Blyth (Yard No.203) as IVY for the Admiralty. *1922* sold to Cia Nav. de los Estados do Mexico SA, Mexico, renamed SINALOA. *1923* renamed NAYARIT. *1926* purchased by The Clan Line Steamers Ltd., name unchanged. *1928* sold to Clarke Steamship Co. Ltd., Quebec, and renamed NORTH VOYAGEUR. *1937* sold to Hellenic Shipping and Commercial Co. Ltd., Greece, and renamed ESPEROS. *21.4.1941* bombed and sunk in Greece.

152. CLAN MACDONALD (3) (1928–1929)
O.N. 160210. 6022 g. 3558 n. 432.2x57.7x28.8 ft.
8-cyl. 4SCDA Burmeister & Wain oil engine by J.G. Kincaid & Co. Ltd., Greenock, 1100nhp.
21.2.1928 launched and *6.1928* completed by Greenock Dockyard Co. Ltd., Greenock (Yard No.414) for The Clan Line Steamers Ltd. *1929* transferred to Scottish Shire Line (Turnbull, Martin & Co. Ltd., managers) and renamed STIRLINGSHIRE. *2.12.1940* torpedoed and sunk by U94 in position 55° 36'N 16° 22'W, 350 miles N.W. of Malin Head on a voyage from Sydney to U.K. via Halifax.

153. CLAN MACDOUGALL (2) (1929–1941)
O.N. 160234. 6843 g. 4079 n. 454.0x62.3x28.9 ft.
8-cyl. 4SCDA Burmeister & Wain oil engine by J.G. Kincaid & Co. Ltd., Greenock, 1100nhp.
28.9.1928 launched and *1.1929* completed by Greenock Dockyard Co. Ltd., Greenock (Yard No.415) for The Clan Line Steamers Ltd. *6.1935* in collision with and sank at Swansea the Danish steamer HJORTHOLM, which was broken up as a result. *31.5.1941* torpedoed and sunk by U106 in position 16° 50'N 25° 10'W, having just sailed from St. Vincent, Cape Verde Islands for the U.K.

154. CLAN MACPHERSON (3) (1929–1943)
O.N. 160249. 6940 g. 4191 n. 454.0x62.3x28.9 ft.
T.3-cyl. with LP exhaust turbine by Rankin & Blackmore Ltd., Glasgow.
9.3.1929 launched and *5.1929* completed by Greenock Dockyard Co. Ltd., Greenock (Yard No.416) for The Clan Line Steamers Ltd. *1.5.1943* torpedoed and sunk by U515 in position 7° 58'N 14° 14'W, 75 miles S.W. of Freetown, having sailed from Takoradi on *26.4.1943* for the U.K.

155. CLAN GRAHAM (3) (1929–1938)
O.N. 132733. 5785 g. 3511 n. 426.0x54.1x37.3 ft.
Q.4-cyl. by N.E. Marine Engineering Co. Ltd., Newcastle, 777nhp.
3.4.1912 launched and *6.1912* completed by Hawthorn, Leslie & Co. Ltd., Hebburn (Yard No.452) as PORT LINCOLN for Commonwealth & Dominion Line Ltd. *1927* sold to C.W. Kellock & Co. Ltd. and renamed CAMBRIAN BARONESS. *1929* purchased by The Clan Line Steamers Ltd. and renamed CLAN GRAHAM. *1938* sold to Neill & Pandelis Ltd., London, and renamed MARITIMA. *2.11.1942* torpedoed and sunk by U522 in position 52° 20'N 45° 40'W, 500 miles N.E. of St. Johns, Newfoundland.

156. CLAN GRANT (3) (1929–1939)
O.N. 135132. 5817 g. 3554 n. 426.0x54.1x37.3 ft.
Q.4-cyl. by N.E. Marine Engineering Co. Ltd., Newcastle, 777nhp.
7.1912 launched and *9.1912* completed by Hawthorn, Leslie & Co. Ltd., Hebburn (Yard No.456) as PORT MACQUARIE for Commonwealth & Dominion Line Ltd. *1927* sold to C.W. Kellock & Co. Ltd. and renamed CAMBRIAN MARCHIONESS. *1929* purchased by The Clan Line Steamers Ltd. and renamed CLAN GRANT. *1939* sold to Stanhope Steamship Co. Ltd., London (J.A. Billmeir, managers) and renamed STANGRANT. *13.10.1940* torpedoed and sunk by U37 in position 58° 27'N 12° 36'W, 220 miles west of Butt of Lewis.

157. CLAN MACALISTER (3) (1930–1940)
O.N. 161909. 6795 g. 4097 n. 453.8x62.3x28.9 ft.
T.3-cyl. with LP exhaust turbine by J.G. Kincaid & Co. Ltd., Greenock, 719nhp.
29.1.1930 launched and *4.1930* completed by Greenock Dockyard Co. Ltd., Greenock (Yard No.418) for The Clan Line Steamers Ltd. *29.5.1940* bombed and sunk off Dunkirk during the evacuation.

158. SINALOA (1931–1933)
O.N. 145240. 1364 g. 627 n. 238.6x36.6x15.6 ft.
T.3-cyl. by Kuy/d Rhee, Rotterdam, 127nhp.
26.3.1921 launched and *5.1921* completed by N.V. Scheepsw de Merwede, Hardinxveld as SANTA GERTRUDIS for San Antonio Steamship Co. Ltd., London (J.S. Evernden, managers). *1925* sold to Cia Nav. de los Estados do Mexico SA, Mexico, and renamed SINALOA. *1931* purchased by The Clan Line Steamers Ltd., name unchanged. *1933* sold to Constantine Marcou Lemos, Syra, Greece, and renamed ARCHON. *21.1.1941* bombed and sunk off the island of Evvia, Greece.

159. CLAN COLQUHOUN (2) (1933–1947)
O.N. 142741. 7914 g. 4888 n. 450.0x58.5x37.1 ft.
Two T.3-cyl. by shipbuilder, twin screw, 1138nhp.
12.12.1918 completed trials by Workman, Clark & Co. Ltd., Belfast (Yard No.436) as WAR ARGUS for the Shipping Controller (White Star Line, managers). *8.1919* sold to Oceanic Steam Navigation Co. Ltd. (White Star Line) and renamed GALLIC. *1933* purchased by The Clan Line Steamers Ltd. and renamed CLAN COLQUHOUN. *1947* sold to Zarati Steamship Co. Ltd., Panama, and renamed IOANNIS LIVANOS. *1949* sold to Dos Oceanos Compagnie de Nav SA, Panama, and renamed JENNY. *1951* sold to Djakarta Lloyd N.V., Indonesia, and renamed IMAN BONDJOL. *1952* renamed DJATINEGARA. *1.12.1955* ashore at Lingayen near Manila after leaking and flooding while in tow from Djakarta to Osaka for scrapping. *21.2.1956* refloated, towed to Manila. *6.1956* scrapped at Osaka.

160. CLAN FARQUHAR (2) (1933–1948)
O.N. 142695. 7958 g. 4897 n. 450.4x58.4x37.2 ft.
Two T.3-cyl. by shipbuilder, twin screw, 1138nhp.
19.9.1918 launched and *31.10.1918* completed as WAR ICARUS by Harland & Wolff Ltd., Belfast (Yard No.540) for The Shipping Controller. *5.1919* sold to Atlantic Transport Co. Ltd. and renamed MESABA. *1925* sold to Oceanic Steam Navigation Co. Ltd. (White Star Line) and renamed DELPHIC. *1933* purchased by The Clan Line Steamers Ltd. and renamed CLAN FARQUHAR. *7.1948* scrapped at Milford Haven.

161. CLAN URQUHART (2) (1933–1936)
O.N. 129581. 9564 g. 5580 n. 526.2x61.4x33.3 ft.
Two Q.4-cyl. by shipbuilder, twin screw, 1264nhp.
27.2.1911 launched and *6.1911* completed by J. Brown & Co., Clydebank (Yard No.399) as ARGYLLSHIRE for Scottish Shire Line (Turnbull, Martin & Co. Ltd., managers). *27.5.1915* missed by two torpedoes from a submarine off Le Havre. *5.2.1917* torpedoed by submarine 3 miles S.W. of Start Point, reached Falmouth safely. *1926* laid-up at Southampton. *1927–1932* laid-up in the Gareloch. *11.2.1932* grounded on Roseneath Spit, Gareloch, while being taken to Glasgow for overhaul prior to returning to service, little damage. *1933* transferred to The Clan Line Steamers Ltd. and renamed CLAN URQUHART. *7.1936* sold to T.W. Ward Ltd. for £22,000 for breaking up at Briton Ferry. *14.3.1937* fire broke out during demolition, vessel scuttled in shallow water.

162. CLAN ROBERTSON (2) (1934–1938)
O.N. 132763. 7951 g. 4954 n. 449.1x58.2x37.1 ft.
Two T.3-cyl. by shipbuilder, twin screw, 1122nhp.
29.10.1919 launched and *2.1920* completed by Barclay, Curle & Co. Ltd., Glasgow (Yard No.574) as OTAKI for New Zealand Shipping Co. Ltd., London, having been laid down as WAR JUPITER. *1934* purchased for £20,000 by The Clan Line Steamers Ltd. and renamed CLAN ROBERTSON. *1938* sold to Stanhope Steamship Co. Ltd. (J.A. Billmeir, managers), London, and renamed STANFLEET. *1939* sold to Zubi Shipping Co. Ltd., London. *12.1939* sold to Blue Star Line Ltd. for £65,000 and renamed PACIFIC STAR. *27.10.1942* torpedoed by U509 N.W. of the Canary Islands in position 29° 15'N 20° 57'W. *28.10.1942* abandoned by her crew at 1740 hours in position 21° 29'N 19° 28'W, and at daylight on *30.10.1942* she was last seen very low in the water and is presumed to have sunk shortly afterwards. She was on a voyage from Rosario and Freetown to Liverpool with 5,037 tons of frozen meat and general cargo, her crew of 86 and 11 gunners were rescued.

163. CLAN MACARTHUR (3) (1936–1943)
O.N. 164066. 10488 g. 6406 n. 477.1x61.2x40.2 ft.
Two T.3-cyl. with LP exhaust turbines by N.E. Marine Engineering Co. Ltd., Newcastle, twin screw, 1152nhp.
14.10.1935 launched and *1.1936* completed by Greenock Dockyard Co. Ltd., Greenock (Yard No.423) for The Clan Line Steamers Ltd. *12.8.1943* torpedoed and sunk by U181 in position 23°S 53° 11'E, 350 miles east of Farafangana, Madagascar, having sailed from Durban on *6.8.1943.*

164. CLAN MACAULAY (2) (1936–1963)
O.N. 164100. 10448 g. 6406 n. 477.1x61.2x40.2 ft.
Two T.3-cyl. with LP exhaust turbines by N.E. Marine Engineering Co. Ltd., Newcastle, twin screw, 1585nhp.
7.8.1936 launched and *11.1936* completed by Greenock Dockyard Co. Ltd., Greenock (Yard No.425) for The Clan Line Steamers Ltd. *19.1.1941* bombed and damaged at Malta. *1960* registered under Houston Line Ltd. *18.11.1963* arrived Dalmuir for scrapping.

165. CLAN CAMERON (3) (1937–1959)
O.N. 164108. 7243 g. 3659 n. 463.7x63.0x29.9 ft.
Two T.3-cyl. with LP exhaust turbines by J.G. Kincaid & Co. Ltd., Greenock, twin screw, 1362nhp.
15.10.1936 launched and *2.1937* completed by Greenock Dockyard Co. Ltd., Greenock (Yard No.426) for The Clan Line Steamers Ltd. *4.3.1959* arrived Hong Kong for scrapping.

166. CLAN CAMPBELL (4) (1937–1942)
O.N. 164112. 7255 g. 3662 n. 463.7x63.0x29.9 ft.
Two T.3-cyl. with LP exhaust turbines by J.G. Kincaid & Co. Ltd., Greenock, twin screw, 1362nhp.
14.1.1937 launched and *4.1937* completed by Greenock Dockyard Co. Ltd., Greenock (Yard No.427) for The Clan Line Steamers Ltd. *13.2.1942* damaged by bombs in position 32° 22'N 24° 22'E, 45 miles N.E. of Tobruk while sailing in a fast convoy of four merchant ships from Alexandria for the relief of Malta. Detached to Tobruk. *23.3.1942* bombed and sunk 8 miles from Filfola Isles, Malta, while sailing in the next fast convoy of four merchant ships from Alexandria.

167. CLAN CHATTAN (2) (1937–1942)
O.N. 165907. 7262 g. 3666 n. 463.7x63.0x29.9 ft.
Two T.3-cyl. with LP exhaust turbines by J.G. Kincaid & Co. Ltd., Greenock, twin screw, 1362nhp.
12.4.1937 launched and *7.1937* completed by Greenock Dockyard Co. Ltd., Greenock (Yard No.428) for The Clan Line Steamers Ltd. *14.2.1942* bombed and sunk in position 35° 01'N 20° 11'E, 190 miles north of Benghazi while sailing in the same Malta convoy as CLAN CAMPBELL. Sunk by an escort.

168. CLAN CHISHOLM (2) (1937–1939)
O.N. 165915. 7256 g. 3671 n. 463.7x63.0x29.9 ft.
Two T.3-cyl. with LP exhaust turbines by J.G. Kincaid & Co. Ltd., Greenock, twin screw, 1362nhp.
5.8.1937 launched and *10.1937* completed by Greenock Dockyard Co. Ltd., Greenock (Yard No.429) for The Clan Line Steamers Ltd. *17.10.1939* torpedoed and sunk by U48 in position 45°N 15°W approx. while homeward bound from India, having sailed in convoy from Gibraltar on *13.10.1939.*

169. CLAN CUMMING (2) (1938–1941)
O.N. 165924. 7264 g. 3676 n. 463.7x63.0x29.9 ft.
Two T.3-cyl. with LP exhaust turbines by J.G. Kincaid & Co. Ltd., Greenock, twin screw, 1370nhp.
18.10.1937 launched and *1.1938* completed by Greenock Dockyard Co. Ltd., Greenock (Yard No.430) for The Clan Line Steamers Ltd. *11.10.1940* damaged by bombing at Liverpool. *19.1.1941* damaged by torpedo off Piraeus, but reached port. *15.4.1941* mined and sunk in the Gulf of Athens.

170. CLAN BUCHANAN (3) (1938–1941)
O.N. 165929. 7266 g. 3692 n. 463.7x63.0x29.9 ft.
Two T.3-cyl. with LP exhaust turbines by J.G. Kincaid & Co. Ltd., Greenock, twin screw, 1370nhp.
21.12.1937 launched and *2.1938* completed by Greenock Dockyard Co. Ltd., Greenock (Yard No.431) for The Clan Line Steamers Ltd. *28.4.1941* sunk by German raider PINGUIN in position 5° 24'N 62° 46'E, Indian Ocean, while on a voyage from Durban to Colombo.

171. CLAN FERGUSON (2) (1938–1942)
O.N. 165937. 7347 g. 3563 n. 463.7x63.0x29.9 ft.
Two T.3-cyl. with LP exhaust turbines by J.G. Kincaid & Co. Ltd., Greenock, twin screw, 1370nhp.
22.3.1938 launched and *6.1938* completed by Greenock Dockyard Co. Ltd., Greenock (Yard No.432) for The Clan Line Steamers Ltd. *21.9.1940* attacked by aircraft at Alexandria. *12.8.1942* torpedoed and sunk by aircraft, 20 miles north of Zembra Island while on a Malta convoy from Gibraltar.

172. CLAN MENZIES (2) (1938–1940)
O.N. 165947. 7336 g. 3555 n. 463.7x63.0x29.9 ft.
Two T.3-cyl. with LP exhaust turbines by J.G. Kincaid & Co. Ltd., Greenock, twin screw, 1370nhp.

15.6.1938 launched and *9.1938* completed by Greenock Dockyard Co. Ltd., Greenock (Yard No.433) for The Clan Line Steamers Ltd. *29.7.1940* sunk by torpedo from U99 in position 54° 10'N 12°W, off the north west coast of Ireland while on a voyage from Melbourne to U.K. ports.

173. CLAN FORBES (3) (1938–1959)
O.N. 165951. 7529 g. 3689 n. 463.7x63.0x29.9 ft.
Two T.3-cyl. with LP exhaust turbines by J.G. Kincaid & Co. Ltd., Greenock, twin screw, 1370nhp.
8.9.1938 launched and *12.1938* completed by Greenock Dockyard Co. Ltd., Greenock (Yard No.434) for The Clan Line Steamers Ltd. *16.8.1940* damaged by bombs in Tilbury Dock. *6.8.1959* arrived at Hong Kong for scrapping.

174. CLAN FRASER (3) (1939–1941)
O.N. 165960. 7529 g. 3524 n. 463.7x63.0x29.9 ft.
Two T.3-cyl. with LP exhaust turbines by J.G. Kincaid & Co. Ltd., Greenock, twin screw, 1370nhp.
20.12.1938 launched and *2.1939* completed by Greenock Dockyard Co. Ltd., Greenock (Yard No.435) for The Clan Line Steamers Ltd. *17.4.1941* bombed by aircraft and exploded with great force while berthed at Piraeus with a cargo of ammunition.

175. CLAN LAMONT (3) (1939–1961)
O.N. 165965. 7673 g. 3524 n. 463.7x63.0x29.9 ft.
Two T.3-cyl. with LP exhaust turbines by J.G. Kincaid & Co. Ltd., Greenock, twin screw, 1370nhp.
22.3.1939 launched and *6.1939* completed by Greenock Dockyard Co. Ltd., Greenock (Yard No.438) for The Clan Line Steamers Ltd. *6.1944* crossed the English Channel five times with invasion troops for Normandy, serving as a Landing Ship Infantry (LSI). *25.7.1944* commissioned into the Royal Navy, renamed H.M.S. LAMONT six days later. *2.8.1944* sailed for the South West Pacific to assist United States Navy, but was rejected and used for training, trooping and an accommodation ship for British Pacific Fleet at Manus, Admiralty Islands. *1946* returned to U.K. via Panama Canal and fitted with extra accommodation for ferrying troops between Tilbury and Cuxhaven. *1947* re-entered Clan Line service. *31.8.1961* arrived Mihara, Japan, for scrapping.

176. CLAN MACDONALD (4) (1939–1970)
O.N. 165971. 9653 g. 5719 n. 481.9x64.7x27.4 ft.
Two 10-cyl. 4SCSA oil engines by J.G. Kincaid & Co. Ltd., Greenock, twin screw, 1631nhp.
15.8.1939 launched and *12.1939* completed by Greenock Dockyard Co. Ltd., Greenock (Yard No.436) for The Clan Line Steamers Ltd. *1.1941* Convoy Commodore ship on Mediterranean convoy to Piraeus. *1960* registered under Houston Line Ltd. *14.3.1966* picked up nine survivors from the tanker WORLD LIBERTY after collision with Norwegian tanker MOSLI in the Red Sea. *6.8.1970* arrived Shanghai for scrapping.

177. CLAN CAMPBELL (5) (1943–1961)
O.N. 168761. 9545 g. 5090 n. 463.8x63.0x38.1 ft.
Two T.3-cyl. with LP exhaust turbines by J.G. Kincaid & Co. Ltd., Greenock, twin screw, 1283nhp.
23.2.1943 launched and *5.1943* completed by Greenock Dockyard Co. Ltd., Greenock (Yard No.453) for The Clan Line Steamers Ltd. *12.1943* rescued 149 survivors from U.S. transport RHONA in Western Mediterranean, landing them at Philippeville, Algeria. *27.9.1961* arrived Hong Kong for scrapping.

178. CLAN URQUHART (3) (1944–1966)
O.N. 169404. 9726 g. 5607 n. 477.0x65.8x37.9 ft.
Two T.3-cyl. with LP exhaust turbines by J.G. Kincaid & Co. Ltd., Greenock, twin screw, 1283nhp.
30.6.1943 launched and *1.1944* completed by Greenock Dockyard Co. Ltd., Greenock (Yard No.454) for The Clan Line Steamers Ltd. and requisitioned for Government service. *1946* entered Clan Line service. *1960* registered under Houston Line Ltd. *8.4.1966* arrived Kaohsiung for scrapping by Chin Ho Fa Steel & Iron Co.

179. CLAN MACDOUGALL (3) (1944–1971)
O.N. 169411. 9710 g. 5556 n. 482.0x64.7x35.6 ft.
Two 10-cyl. 4SCSA oil engines by J.G. Kincaid & Co. Ltd., Greenock, twin screw, 1631nhp.
10.11.1943 launched and *5.1944* completed by Greenock Dockyard Co. Ltd., Greenock (Yard No.455) for the Clan Line Steamers Ltd. *1960* registered under Houston Line Ltd. *1971* sold to Castle Shipping Co. Ltd., Cyprus, and renamed VRYSI. *23.11.1971* left Singapore and arrived Kaohsiung for scrapping prior to *8.12.1971.*

180. CLAN CHATTAN (3) (1944–1962)
O.N. 169413. 9585 g. 5090 n. 463.8x63.0x38.1 ft.
Two T.3-cyl. with LP exhaust turbines by J.G. Kincaid & Co. Ltd., Greenock, twin screw, 1283nhp.
9.3.1944 launched and *6.1944* completed by Greenock Dockyard Co. Ltd., Greenock (Yard No.456) for The Clan Line Steamers Ltd. *9.1950* aground 3 miles north of the Sunk Light Vessel on a voyage from London to Hull. *29.1.1962* registered under King Line Ltd. *14.5.1962* arrived Hong Kong for scrapping.

181. CLAN CHISHOLM (3) (1944–1962)
O.N. 169420. 9581 g. 5083 n. 463.8x63.0x38.1 ft.
Two T.3-cyl. with LP exhaust turbines by J.G. Kincaid & Co. Ltd., Greenock, twin screw, 1283nhp.
23.6.1944 launched and *10.1944* completed by Greenock Dockyard Co. Ltd., Greenock (Yard No.457) for The Clan Line Steamers Ltd. *19.8.1962* arrived Hong Kong for scrapping.

182. CLAN ANGUS (1945–1956) and (1959–1962)
O.N. 166214. 7030 g. 4927 n. 431.3x56.3x35.2 ft.
T.3-cyl. by N.E. Marine Engineering Co. Ltd., Newcastle, 510nhp.

31.3.1942 launched and *5.1942* completed by Caledon Shipbuilding & Engineering Co. Ltd., Dundee (Yard No.394) as EMPIRE PRINCE for the Ministry of War Transport, Gibbs & Co., Newport, appointed managers. *1944* Cayzer Irvine & Co. Ltd. appointed managers. *1945* purchased by The Clan Line Steamers Ltd. and renamed CLAN ANGUS. *1956* registered under Bullard, King & Co. Ltd. and renamed UMKUZI. *1959* registered under Clan Line Steamers Ltd., renamed CLAN ANGUS. *22.4.1962* arrived Hirao for scrapping.

183. CLAN ALPINE (4) (1945–1957) and (1959–1960)
O.N. 169016. 7168 g. 4253 n. 423.8x57.2x34.9 ft.
T.3-cyl. by G. Clark (1938) Ltd., Sunderland, 510nhp.
17.1.1942 launched and *4.1942* completed by J.L. Thompson & Sons Ltd., Sunderland (Yard No.615) as EMPIRE BARRIE for the Ministry of War Transport, Allan, Black & Co., Sunderland, appointed managers. *1944* Cayzer, Irvine & Co. Ltd. appointed managers. *1945* purchased by The Clan Line Steamers Ltd. and renamed CLAN ALPINE. *1952* underwent strain comparison tests with the welded OCEAN VULCAN. *1957* registered under Bullard, King & Co. Ltd. and renamed UMVOTI. *1959* registered under The Clan Line Steamers Ltd. and renamed CLAN ALPINE. *1960* sold to Japanese breakers with delivery *11.1960. 31.10.1960* on passage east caught by cyclone at Chittagong, on voyage Glasgow to Chittagong with general cargo. Driven from moorings and left high and dry in paddy fields at Shonai Chori, 11 miles N.N.W. of entrance to Chittagong River, constructive total loss, cargo discharged into lorries. *14.2.1961* sold to East Bengal Trading Corporation Ltd. and broken up as lay.

184. CLAN MACKINLAY (2) (1946–1962)
O.N. 180221. 7392 g. 5273 n. 431.3x56.3x35.2 ft.
T.3-cyl. by Vickers Armstrong Ltd., Barrow, 541nhp.
25.4.1945 launched and *6.1945* completed by J. Readhead & Sons Ltd., South Shields (Yard No.545) as EMPIRE FAWLEY for the Ministry of War Transport, Cayzer, Irvine & Co. Ltd. appointed managers. *1946* purchased by The Clan Line Steamers Ltd., renamed CLAN MACKINLAY. *2.11.1962* arrived Hong Kong for scrapping.

185. CLAN MACKINNON (3) (1946–1961)
O.N. 180086. 7373 g. 5254 n. 431.3x56.3x35.2 ft.
T.3-cyl. by Central Marine Engine Works, West Hartlepool, 541nhp.
10.7.1945 launched and *9.1945* completed by W. Gray Ltd., West Hartlepool (Yard No.1177) for the Ministry of War Transport as EMPIRE DUNNET, Cayzer, Irvine & Co. Ltd. appointed managers. *1946* purchased by The Clan Line Steamers Ltd. and renamed CLAN MACKINNON. *1955* registered under British and South American Steam Navigation Co. Ltd. (Houston Line, managers). *1957* registered under Houston Line Ltd. (Cayzer, Irvine & Co. Ltd., managers). *1961* sold to Mullion & Co., Hong Kong, renamed ARDROSS. *1963* sold to Concordia Kinabatangan Shipping SA, Panama, and renamed LABUAN BAY. Arrived Kaohsiung for scrapping prior to *9.11.1967.*

186. CLAN MACKAY (5) (1946–1962)
O.N. 180223. 7389 g. 5255 n. 431.2x56.3x35.6 ft.
T.3-cyl. by shipbuilder, 510nhp.

10.8.1945 launched and *11.1945* completed by J. Readhead & Sons Ltd., South Shields (Yard No.547) as EMPIRE GUNFLEET for the Ministry of War Transport. Cayzer, Irvine & Co. Ltd. appointed managers. *1946* purchased by The Clan Line Steamers Ltd., renamed CLAN MACKAY. *1962* sold to Cia de Nav, Victoria Neptuno SA, Panama, and renamed BABYLON. *25.9.1966* arrived Hong Kong for lay-up. *12.1966* delivered to breakers there, and *1.1967* demolition in progress.

187. CLAN ALLAN (1946–1958) and (1959–1961)
O.N. 168653. 7043 g. 4967 n. 430.9x56.2x35.2 ft.
T.3-cyl. by shipbuilders, 510nhp.
15.1.1942 launched and *3.1942* completed by J. Readhead & Sons Ltd., South Shields (Yard No.526) as EMPIRE FOREST for the Ministry of War Transport. Smith, Hogg & Co. appointed managers. *1944* Cayzer, Irvine & Co. Ltd. appointed managers. *1946* purchased by The Clan Line Steamers Ltd. and renamed CLAN ALLAN. *1958* registered under Bullard, King & Co. Ltd., London, renamed UMTALI. *1959* registered under The Clan Line Steamers Ltd., renamed CLAN ALLAN. *1961* sold to Mullion & Co., Hong King, and renamed ARDSIROD. *12.10.1966* arrived Kaohsiung for scrapping.

188. CLAN BRODIE (1946–1963)
O.N. 169474. 7473 g. 3511 n. 463.8x63.0x29.9 ft.
Two T.3-cyl. with LP exhaust turbines by J.G. Kincaid & Co. Ltd., Greenock, twin screw, 1283nhp.
1.10.1940 launched and *10.1941* completed by Greenock Dockyard Co. Ltd., Greenock (Yard No.444) as the seaplane depot ship H.M.S. ATHENE. *1946* purchased by The Clan Line Steamers Ltd., renamed CLAN BRODIE. *19.7.1963* arrived Hong Kong for scrapping.

189. CLAN BUCHANAN (4) (1946–1962)
O.N. 169477. 7467 g. 3511 n. 463.8x63.0x29.9 ft.
Two T.3-cyl. with LP exhaust turbines by J.G. Kincaid & Co. Ltd., Greenock, twin screw, 1283nhp.
11.1941 completed by W. Denny & Brothers Ltd., Dumbarton, as the seaplane carrier H.M.S. ENGADINE. *1946* purchased by The Clan Line Steamers Ltd. and renamed CLAN BUCHANAN. *10.11.1962* arrived Cartagena for scrapping.

190. CLAN CUMMING (3) (1946–1962)
O.N. 169480. 7812 g. 3326 n. 463.8x63.0x29.9 ft.
Two T.3-cyl. with LP exhaust turbines by J.G. Kincaid & Co. Ltd., Greenock, twin screw, 1283nhp.
3.5.1946 launched and *8.1946* completed by Greenock Dockyard Co. Ltd., Greenock (Yard No.459) for The Clan Line Steamers Ltd. *9.1961* first call by a company vessel at Cabinda, Congo, cargo of logs. *18.10.1962* arrived Vigo for scrapping.

191. HESIONE (1946–1948)
O.N. 169050. 7044 g. 4869 n. 430.9x56.2x35.2 ft.
T.3-cyl. by shipbuilder, 510nhp.
20.1.1943 launched and *3.1943* completed by J. Readhead & Sons Ltd., South

Shields (Yard No.532) as EMPIRE CAPULET for the Ministry of War Transport. Cayzer, Irvine & Co. Ltd. appointed managers. *1945* purchased by British and South American Steam Navigation Co. Ltd. (Houston Line, managers) and renamed HESIONE. *1946* registered under The Clan Line Steamers Ltd. *1948* registered under British and South American Steam Navigation Co. Ltd. (Houston Line, managers). *1957* registered under Houston Line Ltd. (Cayzer, Irvine & Co. Ltd., managers). *5.10.1960* arrived Hong Kong for scrapping.

192. CLAN MACRAE (4) (1946–1959)
O.N. 168986. 9209 g. 4922 n. 463.8x63.0x29.9 ft.
Two T.3-cyl. with LP exhaust turbines by J.G. Kincaid & Co. Ltd., Greenock, twin screw, 1372nhp.
17.4.1942 launched and *8.1942* completed by Greenock Dockyard Co. Ltd., Greenock (Yard No.450) as EMPIRE MIGHT for the Ministry of War Transport. Blue Star Line appointed managers. *17.4.1946* purchased by The Clan Line Steamers Ltd., renamed CLAN MACRAE. *1959* registered under Bullard, King & Co. Ltd., London, renamed UMGENI. *1.1960* transferred to Springbok Line, South Africa, and renamed GEMSBOK. *7.1961* transferred to Safmarine, renamed SOUTH AFRICAN FINANCIER. *1962* sold to Spanish shipbreakers, renamed SANTA MARIA DE ORDAZ for the delivery voyage. *10.2.1962* arrived Valencia for scrapping.

193. CLAN MACLAREN (2) (1946–1976)
O.N. 169488. 6389 g. 3344 n. 438.9x60.6x37.9 ft.
6-cyl. 2SCSA oil engine by Barclay, Curle & Co. Ltd., Glasgow, 1291nhp.
25.9.1946 launched and *12.1946* completed by Greenock Dockyard Co. Ltd., Greenock (Yard No.463) for The Clan Line Steamers Ltd. *1976* sold to Seymour Shipping Ltd., London, and renamed SEEMOR. *17.5.1977* arrived Gadani Beach for scrapping.

194. CLAN MACFADYEN (3) (1947–1958)
O.N. 169959. 7176 g. 4380 n. 441.6x56.9x37.4 ft.
T.3-cyl. by Springfield Machinery Co., Springfield, Mass, 2500ihp.
3.1944 completed by New England Shipbuilding Corporation, Portland (Yard No.2224) as SAMDERWENT for the Ministry of War Transport. Cayzer, Irvine & Co. Ltd. appointed managers. *1947* purchased by The Clan Line Steamers Ltd., renamed CLAN MACFADYEN. *1958* sold to Cia Nav. Betacruz SA, Greece, and renamed BETAVISTA. *1968* sold to Thakur Shipping Co. Ltd., India, and renamed VARUNA DEVI. *21.4.1971* arrived Kaohsiung for scrapping.

195. CLAN MACFARLANE (3) (1947–1961)
O.N. 169716. 7176 g. 4380 n. 441.6x56.9x37.4 ft.
T.3-cyl. by Vulcan Iron Works, Wilkes-Barre, Pennsylvania, 2500ihp.
1943 launched as JOHN BRANCH and *8.1943* completed as SAMBRIAN by North Carolina Shipbuilding Corporation, Wilmington (Yard No.186) for the Ministry of War Transport. Cayzer, Irvine & Co. Ltd. appointed managers. *31.8.1946* tail-end shaft and propeller dropped off in the Mediterranean while on a voyage from Alexandria to Naples. Towed by Liberty SAMINVER 7176/44 back to Alexandria, where a new tail-end shaft and propeller were fitted from a wrecked Liberty. *1947* purchased by The Clan Line Steamers Ltd., renamed CLAN MACFARLANE. *1961* sold to Vesta Maritime Corporation, Lebanon, and renamed NICHOLAS. *10.10.1961* aground and

abandoned in a typhoon at Hachinoe, Honshu, while on a voyage from Kamaishi to Vancouver in ballast. *27.10.1961* refloated and towed to Hachinoe Harbour, constructive total loss. *1962* scrapped Yokosuka, arriving *25.1.1962.*

196. CLAN MACLACHLAN (2) (1947–1961)
O.N. 169493. 6365 g. 3178 n. 438.9x60.6x37.9 ft.
3 Steam Turbines by D. Rowan & Co. Ltd., Glasgow, 1440nhp.
23.12.1946 launched and *6.1947* completed by Greenock Dockyard Co. Ltd., Greenock (Yard No.464) for The Clan Line Steamers Ltd. *19.10.1971* arrived Shanghai for scrapping.

197. CLAN MACLEAN (3) (1947–1976)
O.N. 169500. 6009 g. 3328 n. 438.9x60.6x37.9 ft.
6-cyl. 2SCSA oil engine by Barclay, Curle & Co. Ltd., Glasgow, 1291nhp.
2.6.1947 launched and *10.1947* completed by Greenock Dockyard Co. Ltd. (Yard No.465) for The Clan Line Steamers Ltd. *1956* rescued crew of sail training ship MOYANA off the Lizard. *1976* sold to Singapore Islands (Pte) Ltd., Singapore, and renamed SENTOSA ISLAND. *8.5.1979* arrived Kaohsiung for scrapping.

198. CLAN MACLENNAN (1947–1971)
O.N. 182080. 6366 g. 3168 n. 438.9x60.6x37.9 ft.
3 Steam Turbines by D. Rowan & Co. Ltd., Glasgow, 1440nhp.
16.9.1947 launched and *12.1947* completed by Greenock Dockyard Co. Ltd., Greenock (Yard No.466) for The Clan Line Steamers Ltd. *2.12.1961* in collision with tanker BRITISH DEFENDER 6138/50 off Beira, arrived Beira next day. *24.11.1966* in collision with tanker BRITISH CRUSADER 11346/54 in fog near No.9 Barrow Buoy, Thames Estuary, repaired at South Shields. *16.9.1971* arrived Shanghai for scrapping.

199. CLAN DAVIDSON (2) (1948–1962)
O.N. 182100. 8067 g. 3697 n. 463.8x63.0x29.9 ft.
Two T.3-cyl. with LP exhaust turbines by J.G. Kincaid & Co. Ltd., Greenock, twin screw, 1283nhp.
27.10.1942 launched and *1.1943* completed as H.M.S. BONAVENTURE, having been purchased while on the stocks by the Admiralty. *23.1.1943* commissioned as a depot-ship for midget submarines in Scottish waters for operations against enemy-controlled Norway. *2.1943* blown ashore at Castle Toward from her anchorage in Rothesay Bay, ending up close to rows of tied-up conventional submarines. *21.2.1945* sailed to Far East for midget submarine operations against the Japanese. *5.1947* returned to the U.K. *1948* entered Clan Line service as CLAN DAVIDSON. *25.12.1961* arrived Hong Kong for scrapping.

200. CLAN KEITH (2) (1948–1961)
O.N. 167858. 7174 g. 4272 n. 425.1x57.0x34.8 ft.
T.3-cyl. by General Machinery Corporation, Hamilton, Ohio, 505nhp.
6.1942 completed by Permanente Metals Corporation Shipyard No.1, Richmond, California (Yard No.24) as OCEAN VERITY for the Ministry of War Transport. Glen Line Ltd. appointed managers. *1948* purchased by The Clan Line Steamers Ltd., renamed CLAN KEITH. *5.11.1961* broke in two 11 miles south of Galita Island off

the coast of Tunisia after striking the Ecueils des Sorelles Rocks, near Cape Bon, on a voyage from U.K. to Colombo via Malta with general cargo. The after part sank later the same day and the forward section sank the following morning. There were only six survivors from a crew of 68, five of which were picked up by the British DURHAM TRADER 6214/59.

201. CLAN MACBRIDE (2) (1948–1958)
O.N. 169067. 7174 g. 4272 n. 425.1x57.0x34.8 ft.
T.3-cyl. by J. Inglis, Ontario, 505nhp.
11.1942 completed by Todd-Bath Shipbuilders, Portland, Maine (Yard No.29) as OCEAN GYPSY for the Ministry of War Transport (J. & C. Harrison, managers). *1948* purchased by The Clan Line Steamers Ltd. *1958* sold to Valles Steamship Co., Panama (Wheelock, Marden & Co., managers) and renamed ALICE. *7.10.1966* arrived Hirao for scrapping.

202. CLAN KENNETH (2) (1948–1958)
O.N. 168734. 7174 g. 4272 n. 425.1x57.0x34.8 ft.
T.3-cyl. by General Machinery Corporation, Hamilton, Ohio, 505nhp.
6.1942 completed by Permanente Metals Corporation Shipyard No.1, Richmond, California (Yard No.25) as OCEAN VICEROY for The Ministry of War Transport. P. Henderson & Co. appointed managers. *29.3.1943* damaged by submarine torpedo in mid-Atlantic. *1948* purchased by The Clan Line Steamers Ltd. and renamed CLAN KENNETH. *12.8.1953* towed motor yacht ADVENTURESS, immobilised in the Bay of Biscay, into Falmouth. *1958* sold to Concordia de Nay SA, Greece, and renamed OMONIA II. *13.4.1966* beached at Amsterdam after arriving on fire from Djakarta. *15.7.1966* arrived in tow at Hamburg for scrapping.

203. CLAN MACBRAYNE (2) (1948–1961)
O.N. 168638. 7129 g. 4252 n. 425.1x57.0x34.8 ft.
T.3-cyl. by J. Inglis, Ontario, 505nhp.
10.1942 completed by Todd-Bath Shipbuilders, Portland, Maine (Yard No.25) as OCEAN MESSENGER for the Ministry of War Transport. Watts, Watts & Co. appointed managers. *1948* purchased by The Clan Line Steamers Ltd., renamed CLAN MACBRAYNE. *1960* registered under King Line Ltd. *27.3.1961* arrived Mihara, Japan, for scrapping, sold for £65,000.

204. CLAN MACBEAN (2) (1948–1960)
O.N. 168840. 7129 g. 4250 n. 425.1x57.0x34.8 ft.
T.3-cyl. by Dominion Engineering Works, Montreal, 505nhp.
10.1942 completed by Todd-Bath Shipbuilders, Portland, Maine (Yard No.24) as OCEAN COURIER for the Ministry of War Transport. Larrinaga Steamship Co., Liverpool, appointed managers. *30.7.1944* damaged by E-boat torpedo in the English Channel. *1948* purchased by The Clan Line Steamers Ltd. and renamed CLAN MACBEAN. *20.8.1960* arrived Hong Kong for scrapping, sold for £59,000.

205. CLAN KENNEDY (2) (1948–1959)
O.N. 165840. 7129 g. 4272 n. 425.1x57.0x34.8 ft.
T.3-cyl. by General Machinery Corporation, Hamilton, Ohio, 505nhp.

6.1942 completed by Permanente Metals Corporation, Shipyard No.1, Richmond, California (Yard No.23) as OCEAN VISCOUNT for the Ministry of War Transport. Bibby Brothers appointed managers. *1948* purchased by The Clan Line Steamers Ltd., renamed CLAN KENNEDY. *1959* sold to Eddie Steamship Co. Ltd., Keelung, and renamed KELLY. *1960* scrapped in Japan.

206. CLAN MACBETH (2) (1948–1959)
O.N. 169176. 7178 g. 4325 n. 425.1x57.0x34.8 ft.
T.3-cyl. by J. Inglis, Ontario, 505nhp.
11.1942 completed by Todd-Bath Shipbuilders, Portland, Maine (Yard No.30) as OCEAN GLORY for the Ministry of War Transport. J. & C. Harrison, London, appointed managers. *1946* Cayzer, Irvine & Co. Ltd. appointed managers. *1948* purchased by The Clan Line Steamers Ltd. and renamed CLAN MACBETH. *1959* sold to Panamanian Oriental Steamship Corporation, Panama (Wheelock, Marden & Co., managers) and renamed MADONNA. *1961* sold to Sincere Navigation Corporation, Keelung, Taiwan, and renamed SINCERE TRADER. *12.1964* scrapped at Kaohsiung.

207. CLAN MACKENZIE (4) (1948–1960)
O.N. 168949. 7025 g. 4850 n. 431.5x56.3x35.2 ft.
T.3-cyl. by Central Marine Engine Works, West Hartlepool, 510nhp.
10.11.1942 launched and *30.12.1942* completed by W. Gray & Co. Ltd., West Hartlepool (Yard No.1138) as EMPIRE CATO for the Ministry of War Transport. The Hain Steamship Co. Ltd. appointed managers. *12.4.1946* chartered to The Clan Line Steamers Ltd. for three years under the Ministry's Ship Disposal Scheme and delivered at 1700 hours at Barrow. *31.12.1947* purchased by The Clan Line Steamers Ltd. *1948* Renamed CLAN MACKENZIE. *1960* sold to Wheelock, Marden & Co. Ltd. for demolition and arrived *14.10.1960* at Hong Kong. *11.1960* demolition commenced.

208. CLAN MACKENDRICK (1948–1961)
O.N. 169053. 7054 g. 4851 n. 430.9x56.2x35.2 ft.
T.3-cyl. by shipbuilder, 542nhp.
31.8.1943 launched and *11.1943* completed by J. Readhead & Sons Ltd., South Shields (Yard No.536) as EMPIRE PICKWICK for the Ministry of War Transport. Donaldson Brothers & Black appointed managers. *1946* Cayzer, Irvine & Co. Ltd. appointed managers. *1948* purchased by The Clan Line Steamers Ltd. and renamed CLAN MACKENDRICK. *1961* sold to Mullion & Co., Hong Kong, and renamed ARDPATRICK. *1966* sold to National Shipping Corporation, Pakistan, and renamed HARINGHATA. *16.7.1968* arrived Karachi for scrapping.

209. CLAN MACKELLAR (2) (1948–1961)
O.N. 180071. 7067 g. 4844 n. 431.5x56.2x35.2 ft.
T.3-cyl. by Central Marine Engine Works, West Hartlepool, 510nhp.
24.2.1944 launched and *4.1944* completed by W. Gray & Co. Ltd., West Hartlepool (Yard No.1161) as EMPIRE LANKESTER for the Ministry of War Transport. J. Robinson & Sons, North Shields, appointed managers. *1946* Cayzer Irvine & Co. Ltd. appointed managers. *1948* purchased by The Clan Line Steamers Ltd., renamed CLAN MACKELLAR. *1961* sold to Mullion & Co., Hong Kong, and renamed ARDGROOM. *20.2.1967* arrived Hong Kong for scrapping by Lee Sing Co.

210. CLAN MACLEOD (4) (1948–1976)
O.N. 182090. 5997 g. 3240 n. 438.9x60.6x37.9 ft.
6-cyl. 2SCSA oil engine by Barclay, Curle & Co. Ltd., Glasgow, 1290nhp.
13.2.1948 launched and *7.1948* completed by Greenock Dockyard Co. Ltd., Greenock (Yard No.467) for The Clan Line Steamers Ltd. *1976* sold to Alligator Shipping Co. Ltd., Cyprus, for $610,000 and renamed PAPAJI. *14.3.1978* arrived Gadani Beach for scrapping.

211. CLAN MACLAY (1949–1971)
O.N. 182109. 6388 g. 3367 n. 438.9x60.6x37.9 ft.
6-cyl. 2SCSA oil engine by Barclay, Curle & Co. Ltd., Glasgow, 1290nhp.
7.5.1948 launched and *3.1949* completed by Greenock Dockyard Co. Ltd., Greenock (Yard No.468) for The Clan Line Steamers Ltd. *1976* sold to Climax Shipping Corporation, Panama, and renamed CLIMAX AMETHYST. *1979* sold to Panama flag interests and renamed ANGELOS for the voyage Singapore to a Kaohsiung scrapyard, arriving prior to *15.6.1979.*

212. CLAN MACTAGGART (2) (1949–1971)
O.N. 182111. 8035 g. 3924 n. 470.0x65.6x40.9 ft.
6 Parsons steam turbines by J.G. Kincaid & Co. Ltd., Greenock, DR geared to two screw shafts, 9400shp.
8.10.1948 launched and *3.1949* completed by Greenock Dockyard Co. Ltd., Greenock (Yard No.469) for The Clan Line Steamers Ltd. *21.4.1964* in collision with the Dutch TJIPONDOK 7646/45 while manoeuvering to moor at No.2 buoy at Beira. *12.11.1971* arrived Bilbao for scrapping.

213. CLAN MACTAVISH (3) (1949–1971)
O.N. 182124. 8035 g. 3924 n. 470.0x65.6x40.9 ft.
6 parsons steam turbines by J.G. Kincaid & Co. Ltd., Greenock, DR geared to two screw shafts, 9400shp.
2.3.1949 launched and *6.1949* completed by Greenock Dockyard Co. Ltd., Greenock (Yard No.470) for The Clan Line Steamers Ltd. *22.10.1971* arrived Whampoa for scrapping.

214. CLAN SHAW (3) (1949–1960)
O.N. 182140. 8101 g. 4659 n. 488.9x66.3x29.6 ft.
3 Parsons steam turbines by J.G. Kincaid & Co. Ltd., Greenock, DR geared to two screw shafts, 10340shp.
23.8.1949 launched by Lady Rotherwick and *12.1949* completed by Greenock Dockyard Co. Ltd., Greenock (Yard No.471) for The Clan Line Steamers Ltd. *1.1960* transferred to Springbok Line, South Africa, and renamed STEENBOK. *7.1961* transferred to Safmarine, renamed SOUTH AFRICAN SEAFARER. *1966* renamed S.A. SEAFARER. *1.7.1966* aground while entering Table Bay from Glasgow near the Green Point Lighthouse, 63 crew and 12 passengers taken off by helicopter. Wreck broke up and was scrapped locally.

215. CLAN SINCLAIR (3) (1950–1960)
O.N. 182148. 8386 g. 4555 n. 488.9x66.3x29.6 ft.
3 Parsons steam turbines by J.G. Kincaid & Co. Ltd., Greenock, DR geared to two screw shafts, 10340shp.

17.1.1950 launched and *4.1950* completed by Greenock Dockyard Co. Ltd., Greenock (Yard No.472) for The Clan Line Steamers Ltd. *1.1960* transferred to Springbok Line, South Africa, and renamed BOSBOK. *7.1961* transferred to Safmarine, renamed SOUTH AFRICAN STATESMAN. *1966* renamed S.A. STATESMAN. *3.11.1972* arrived Kaohsiung for scrapping.

216. CLAN MACQUARRIE (2) (1951–1953)
O.N. 168636. 7131 g. 4252 n. 425.1x57.0x34.8 ft.
T.3-cyl. by Canadian Allis Chalmers, Montreal, 505nhp.
9.1942 completed by Todd-Bath Shipbuilding Corporation, Portland, Maine (Yard No.19) as OCEAN WAYFARER for the Ministry of War Transport. Thompson Steamshipping Co., Cardiff, appointed managers. *1951* purchased by The Clan Line Steamers Ltd. and renamed CLAN MACQUARRIE. *31.1.1953* ashore 10 miles to the west of Butt of Lewis while on a voyage from Dundee to Glasgow. *16.3.1953* refloated, constructive total loss. *29.10.1953* arrived at West of Scotland Shipbreakers Ltd., Troon, for scrapping.

217. CLAN MACQUEEN (1951–1954)
O.N. 168630. 7174 g. 4272 n. 425.1x57.0x34.8 ft.
T.3-cyl. by General Machinery Corporation, Hamilton, Ohio, 505nhp.
1.1942 completed by Permanente Metals Corporation, Shipyard No.1, Richmond, California (Yard No.6), as OCEAN VESPER for the Ministry of War Transport. Kaye, Son & Co. appointed managers. *1942* Connell & Grace Ltd., Newcastle, appointed managers. *1946* Thompson Steamshipping Co., Cardiff, appointed managers. *1951* purchased by The Clan Line Steamers Ltd. and renamed CLAN MACQUEEN. *1954* registered under British and South American Steam Navigation Co. Ltd. (Houston Line Ltd., managers) and renamed HERMINIUS. *1958* sold to Pan Norse Steamship Co. SA, Panama, and renamed EKBERG. *11.12.1964* arrived Onomichi for scrapping.

218. HELLENES (1951–1952) and (1957–1958)
O.N. 168815. 7174 g. 4272 n. 425.1x57.0x34.8 ft.
T.3-cyl. by General Machinery Corporation, Hamilton, Ohio, 505nhp.
1.1942 completed by Todd-California Shipbuilding Corporation, Richmond, California (Yard No.8) as OCEAN VESTAL for the Ministry of War Transport. Kaye, Son & Co. appointed managers. *18.11.1946* sold to Thompson Steamshipping Co. Ltd., Cardiff. *1947* renamed FARNINGHAM. *1951* purchased by The Clan Line Steamers Ltd. *1952* registered under British and South American Steam Navigation Co. Ltd. (Houston Line, managers) and renamed HELLENES. *1957* registered under The Clan Line Steamers Ltd. *1958* sold to Malabar Steamship Co. Ltd., India, and renamed JANMADA. *15.4.1962* demolition commenced at Bombay.

219. CLAN SUTHERLAND (2) (1951–1971)
O.N. 182167. 8436 g. 4434 n. 488.9x66.3x29.6 ft.
3 Parsons steam turbines by J.G. Kincaid & Co. Ltd., Greenock, DR geared to a single screw shaft, 10340shp.
28.12.1950 launched by Duchess of Sutherland and *3.1951* completed by Greenock Dockyard Co. Ltd., Greenock (Yard No.475) for The Clan Line Steamers Ltd. *10.11.1971* arrived HsingKiang for scrapping.

220. CLAN MACINTOSH (3) (1951–1978)
O.N. 184959. 6454 g. 3605 n. 438.9x60.6x37.9 ft.
6-cyl. 2SCSA oil engine by shipbuilder, 6000bhp.
19.7.1951 launched and *11.1951* completed by J. Brown & Co. Ltd., Clydebank (Yard No.665) for The Clan Line Steamers Ltd. *1978* sold to Sanil Shipping Co., Hong King, for $350,000 and renamed SANIL. *30.8.1980* arrived Bombay breakers.

221. CLAN MACINTYRE (3) (1952–1976)
O.N. 184963. 6399 g. 3602 n. 438.9x60.6x37.9 ft.
6-cyl. 2SCSA oil engine by shipbuilder, 6000bhp.
31.10.1951 launched by Lady Rotherwick and *3.1952* completed by J. Brown & Co. Ltd., Clydebank (Yard No.666) for The Clan Line Steamers Ltd. *1976* sold to Renown Bay Shipping Co. Ltd., Panama, and renamed EASTERN EXPRESS. *22.12.1979* aground south of La Spezia at Marina di Carrara after leaving La Spezia for Sardinia, total loss.

222. CLAN MACINNES (3) (1952–1978)
O.N. 184974. 6517 g. 3621 n. 438.9x60.6x37.9 ft.
6-cyl. 2SCSA oil engine by J. Brown & Co. Ltd., Clydebank, 6400bhp.
9.4.1952 launched and *7.1952* completed by Greenock Dockyard Co. Ltd., Greenock (Yard No.478) for The Clan Line Steamers Ltd. *1978* sold to Ali Khalifa Mirchandani Shipping Co. Ltd. for $350,000 and renamed ATHOUB. *15.10.1979* arrived Kaohsiung breakers.

223. CLAN STEWART (1954–1961) and (1962–1967)
O.N. 185001. 8163 g. 4587 n. 488.9x66.3x29.6 ft.
3 Parsons steam turbines by J.G. Kincaid & Co. Ltd., Greenock, DR geared to a single screw shaft, 10340shp.
22.10.1953 launched and *2.1954* completed by Greenock Dockyard Co. Ltd., Greenock (Yard No.481) for The Clan Line Steamers Ltd. *1961* transferred to Safmarine and renamed SOUTH AFRICAN SCULPTOR. *1962* transferred back to The Clan Line Steamers Ltd. and renamed KINPURNIE CASTLE. *1967* sold to Astro Firme SA, Panama, and renamed HELLENIC MED. *15.3.1978* arrived Gadani Beach for scrapping.

224. CLAN ROBERTSON (3) (1954–1959)
O.N. 185012. 7878 g. 4107 n. 465.9x65.6x39.7 ft.
3 Parsons steam turbines by J.G. Kincaid & Co. Ltd., Greenock, DR geared to a single screw shaft, 9400shp.
17.3.1954 launched by Mrs Anthony Cayzer and *6.1954* completed by Greenock Dockyard Co. Ltd., Greenock (Yard No.482) for The Clan Line Steamers Ltd. *1959* registered under Bullard, King & Co., London, and renamed UMZINTO. *1.1960* transferred to Springbok Line, South Africa, and renamed ROOIBOK. *7.1961* transferred to Safmarine, renamed SOUTH AFRICAN SHIPPER. *1966* renamed S.A. SHIPPER. *26.11.1975* arrived Kaohsiung for scrapping.

225. CLAN ROSS (3) (1956–1961) and (1962–1975)
O.N. 185040. 7775 g. 4256 n. 465.0x65.6x39.7 ft.
3 Parsons steam turbine by J.G. Kincaid & Co. Ltd., Greenock, DR geared to a single screw shaft, 9400shp.

17.1.1956 launched by Miss Nichola Cayzer and *4.1956* completed by Greenock Dockyard Co. Ltd., Greenock (Yard No.487) for The Clan Line Steamers Ltd. *1961* transferred to Safmarine and renamed SOUTH AFRICAN SCIENTIST. *1962* transferred back to The Clan Line Steamers Ltd. and renamed KINNAIRD CASTLE. *1969* registered under King Line Ltd. *1975* sold to Dasonab Nav SA, Panama, and renamed NAZEER. *26.4.1978* arrived Gadani Beach for scrapping.

226. ARGYLLSHIRE (1956–1975)
O.N. 185047. 9299 g. 5267 n. 470.8x69.3x28.4 ft.
3 Parsons steam turbines by J.G. Kincaid & Co. Ltd., Greenock, DR geared to a single screw shaft, 11550shp.
23.5.1956 launched by Countess Jellicoe and *10.1956* completed by Greenock Dockyard Co. Ltd., Greenock (Yard No.486) for The Clan Line Steamers Ltd. *1960* registered under Scottish Shire Line. *1975* sold to Gulf East Marine Ltd. and renamed SCHIVAGO. *3.8.1977* arrived Gadani Beach for scrapping.

227. AYRSHIRE (1957–1965)
O.N. 300171. 9360 g. 5302 n. 470.8x69.3x28.4 ft.
3 Parsons steam turbines by J.G. Kincaid & Co. Ltd., Greenock, DR geared to a single screw shaft, 11550shp.
19.10.1956 launched by Countess of Powis and *5.1957* completed by Greenock Dockyard Co. Ltd., Greenock (Yard No.488) for The Clan Line Steamers Ltd. *1960* registered under Scottish Shire Line. *23.3.1965* aground at Abd Al Awi, 430 miles E.S.E. of Aden near Socotra while on a voyage from Liverpool to Brisbane. *26.4.1965* refloated briefly but ran aground again, and salvage abandoned the next day.

228. CLAN MALCOLM (2) (1957–1979)
O.N. 300181. 7326 g. 3717 n. 465.0x65.6x39.7 ft.
6-cyl. 2SCSA Doxford oil engine by Wallsend Slipway & Engineering Co. Ltd., Wallsend, 8000bhp.
29.4.1957 launched by Mrs Malcolm and *8.1957* completed by Greenock Dockyard Co. Ltd., Greenock (Yard No.490) for The Clan Line Steamers Ltd. *1979* sold to Bective Shipping Co., Panama, for $1m with CLAN MENZIES en-bloc, renamed TRINITY FAIR. *25.5.1979* left Bangkok for Shanghai for scrapping.

229. CLAN MATHESON (5) (1957–1978)
O.N. 300186. 7315 g. 3715 n. 465.0x65.6x39.7 ft.
6-cyl. 2SCSA Doxford oil engine by Wallsend Slipway & Engineering Co. Ltd., Wallsend, 8000bhp.
26.8.1957 launched and *12.1957* completed by Greenock Dockyard Co. Ltd., Greenock (Yard No.489) for The Clan Line Steamers Ltd. *12.12.1978* arrived Kaohsiung breakers.

230. CLAN MENZIES (3) (1958–1979)
O.N. 300200. 7315 g. 3714 n. 465.0x65.6x39.7 ft.
6-cyl. 2SCSA Doxford oil engine by Wallsend Slipway & Engineering Co. Ltd., Wallsend, 8000bhp.
22.1.1958 launched by Mrs Macdonald and *5.1958* completed by Greenock Dockyard Co. Ltd., Greenock (Yard No.491) for The Clan Line Steamers Ltd. *1979*

sold to Bective Shipping Co., Panama, for $1m with CLAN MALCOLM en-bloc, and renamed TRINITY SPLENDOUR. *1980* sold to China Ocean Shipping Co., Hebei, China, and renamed XING LONG.

231. CLAN MACIVER (3) (1958–1979)
O.N. 300214. 7105 g. 3695 n. 455.0x61.6x38.8 ft.
5-cyl. 2SCSA Doxford oil engine by Barclay, Curle & Co. Ltd., Glasgow, 5400bhp.
23.6.1958 launched by Mrs J.A. Thomson and *11.1958* completed by Greenock Dockyard Co. Ltd., Greenock (Yard No.492) for The Clan Line Steamers Ltd. *1979* sold to Quin Ace Maritime SA, Panama, and renamed TRINITY PRIDE. *9.2.1980* arrived Shanghai breakers.

232. CLAN MACINDOE (2) (1959–1979)
O.N. 301401. 8991 g. 4874 n. 455.0x61.6x38.8 ft.
5-cyl. Doxford 2SCSA oil engine by shipbuilder, 5400bhp.
20.8.1959 launched by Mrs Elvish and *11.1959* completed by J. Brown & Co. Ltd., Clydebank (Yard No.712) for Neptune Shipping Co. Ltd., Hamilton (Cayzer, Irvine & Co. Ltd., managers). *1979* sold to Gulf Shipping Lines Ltd. and renamed GULF HERON. *9.1980* aground and damaged by shelling at Basrah.

233. CLAN MURDOCH (2) (1960–1962)
O.N. 180865. 7375 g. 4738 n. 425.9x56.0x38.1 ft.
T.3-cyl. by N.E. Marine Engineering Co. Ltd., Sunderland.
16.1.1946 launched by Bartram & Sons Ltd., Sunderland (Yard No.306) as EMPIRE SOUTHWOLD for the Ministry of War Transport. *5.1946* completed as HESPERIA for British and South American Steam Navigation Co. Ltd. (Houston Line Ltd., managers). *1957* registered under Houston Line Ltd. (Cayzer, Irvine & Co. Ltd., managers). *11.10.1960* registered under The Clan Line Steamers Ltd. and renamed CLAN MURDOCH. *1962* sold to Sadikzade Rusen O.K., Sirketi, Turkey, and renamed MUSTAFA. *1974* sold to Denizhanlar Vapuru Donatua Istiraki, Turkey, and renamed DENIZHANLAR. *3.1979* arrived Aliga-Lizmir, Turkey, for scrapping.

234. CLAN MURRAY (4) (1960–1962)
O.N. 180929. 7301 g. 4663 n. 425.9x56.0x38.1 ft.
T.3-cyl. by G. Clark Ltd., Sunderland.
2.5.1946 launched by Shipbuilding Corporation Ltd., Sunderland (Yard No.9) as EMPIRE LONGSTONE for the Ministry of War Transport. *8.1946* completed as HESPERIDES for British and South American Steam Navigation Co. Ltd. (Houston Line Ltd., managers). *1957* registered under Houston Line Ltd. (Cayzer, Irvine & Co. Ltd., managers). *1960* registered under The Clan Line Steamers Ltd. and renamed CLAN MURRAY. *1962* scrapped at Osaka.

235. CLAN MACILWRAITH (2) (1960–1979)
O.N. 301428. 6894 g. 3701 n. 455.0x61.6x38.8 ft.
5-cyl. 2SCSA Doxford oil engine by Wallsend Slipway & Engineering Co. Ltd., Wallsend, 5400bhp.
27.5.1960 launched by Mrs Anthony Cayzer and *12.1960* completed by Greenock Dockyard Co. Ltd., Greenock (Yard No.496) for The Clan Line Steamers Ltd. *1979* sold to Guan Guan Shipping (Pte) Ltd., Singapore, and renamed GOLDEN CITY.

17.7.1986 on fire in No.1 hold in Malacca Strait in position 5° 02'N 97° 58'E while on a voyage from Colombo to Singapore. *24.7.1986* arrived Singapore and cargo discharged, total loss. *21.10.1986* demolition commenced by National Shipbreakers (Pte) Ltd. at Jurong, Singapore.

236. CLAN FERGUSSON (1961–1965)
O.N. 301439. 9292 g. 4993 n. 461.0x62.3x37.6 ft.
6-cyl. 2SCSA Sulzer oil engine by Wallsend Slipway & Engineering Co. Ltd., Wallsend, 7700bhp.
3.11.1960 launched by Mrs H.S. Cayzer and *4.1961* completed by Swan, Hunter & Wigham Richardson Ltd., Wallsend (Yard No.1917) for The Clan Line Steamers Ltd. *1965* sold to Scindia Line, India, and renamed JALAPANKHI. *5.2.1983* arrived Bombay breakers.

237. CLAN MACNAB (4) (1961–1980)
O.N. 301448. 9169 g. 4995 n. 468.0x61.6x38.1 ft.
6-cyl. 2SCSA Doxford oil engine by Wallsend Slipway & Engineering Co. Ltd., Wallsend, 6400bhp.
31.1.1961 launched by Countess Jellicoe and *5.1961* completed by Greenock Dockyard Co. Ltd., Greenock (Yard No.497) for The Clan Line Steamers Ltd. *1980* sold to New Eagle Navigation SA, Panama, and renamed NEW EAGLE. *1.11.1984* arrived Shanghai breakers.

238. CLAN FORBES (4) (1961–1968)
O.N. 301454. 9240 g. 4995 n. 461.0x62.3x37.6 ft.
6-cyl. 2SCSA Sulzer oil engine by Wallsend Slipway & Engineering Co. Ltd., Wallsend, 7700bhp.
2.3.1961 launched by Mrs A.E Lemon and *6.1961* completed by Swan, Hunter & Wigham Richardson Ltd., Wallsend (Yard No.1919) for The Clan Line Steamers Ltd. *1968* sold to Arya National Shipping Line, Iran, and renamed ARYA MAN. *1980* renamed IRAN HEMMET by Iran Shipping Lines. *3.10.1985* arrived breakers at Alang, India.

239. CLAN FRASER (4) (1961–1965)
O.N. 301461. 9292 g. 4992 n. 461.0x62.3x37.6 ft.
6-cyl. 2SCSA Sulzer oil engine by Wallsend Slipway & Engineering Co. Ltd., Wallsend, 7700bhp.
27.7.1961 launched by Mrs G.F. Bedford and *9.1961* completed by Swan, Hunter & Wigham Richardson Ltd., Wallsend (Yard No.1921) for The Clan Line Steamers Ltd. *1965* sold to Scindia Line, India, and renamed JALAPALAKA. *20.11.1979* on fire at Bombay and subsequently broken up there.

240. CLAN GRAHAM (4) (1962–1981)
O.N. 301465. 9022 g. 5104 n. 461.0x62.3x37.6 ft.
6-cyl. 2SCSA Sulzer oil engine by Barclay, Curle & Co. Ltd., Glasgow, 7700bhp.
25.8.1961 launched by Mrs R.J. Bloxam and *1.1962* completed by Greenock Dockyard Co. Ltd., Greenock (Yard No.498) for The Clan Line Steamers Ltd. *1969* registered under King Line Ltd. *1977* registered under The Clan Line Steamers Ltd. *1981* sold to Scan Maritime Co. Ltd., Panama, and renamed MARIANNE. *1983* sold to Kinsdale International SA, Panama, and renamed CANDELARIA. *23.3.1984* arrived Kaohsiung breakers.

241. CLAN MACNAIR (2) (1962–1980)
O.N. 301468. 9137 g. 4928 n. 468.0x61.6x38.1 ft.
6-cyl. 2SCSA Doxford oil engine by shipbuilder, 6400bhp.
26.10.1961 launched by Lady Aberconway and *2.1962* completed by J. Brown & Co. Ltd., Clydebank (Yard No.713) for Neptune Shipping Co. Ltd., Hamilton (Cayzer, Irvine & Co. Ltd., managers). *1980* sold to Uni-Ocean Lines (Pte) Ltd., Singapore, and renamed LICHIANG. *7.4.1987* arrived Kaohsiung breakers.

242. CLAN FARQUHARSON (1962–1968)
O.N. 301475. 9240 g. 4993 n. 461.0x62.3x37.6 ft.
6-cyl. 2SCSA Sulzer oil engine by Wallsend Slipway & Engineering Co. Ltd., Wallsend, 7700bhp.
19.1.1962 launched by Lady Doreen Prior-Palmer and *4.1962* completed by Swan, Hunter & Wigham Richardson Ltd., Wallsend (Yard No.1931) for The Clan Line Steamers Ltd. *1968* sold to Arya National Shipping Line, Iran, and renamed ARYA SEP. *1980* renamed IRAN OKHUVAT by Iran Shipping Lines. *1983* renamed OKHUVAT by Irano-Hind Shipping Co. Ltd. *24.9.1985* anchored off Mangalore, India, for scrapping.

243. CLAN GRANT (4) (1962–1981)
O.N. 301480. 9022 g. 4804 n. 461.0x62.3x37.6 ft.
6-cyl. 2SCSA Sulzer oil engine by Barclay, Curle & Co. Ltd., Glasgow, 7700bhp.
22.12.1961 launched by Mrs H.E. Gorick and *5.1962* completed by Greenock Dockyard Co. Ltd., Greenock (Yard No.499) for The Clan Line Steamers Ltd. *1969* registered under King Line Ltd. *1977* registered under The Clan Line Steamers Ltd. *1981* sold to Venables Steamship SA, Panama, and renamed ENRIQUETA. *16.1.1985* arrived Chinese breakers.

244. CLAN MACGILLIVRAY (2) (1962–1981)
O.N. 304140. 8811 g. 4813 n. 471.0x63.0x37.7 ft.
6-cyl. 2SCSA Sulzer oil engine by Barclay, Curle & Co. Ltd., Glasgow, 8500bhp.
22.5.1962 launched by Mrs G.H. Mayhew and *9.1962* completed by Greenock Dockyard Co. Ltd., Greenock (Yard No.500) for The Clan Line Steamers Ltd. *1969* registered under King Line Ltd. *1977* registered under The Clan Line Steamers Ltd. *1981* sold to Gateway Shipping Ltd., Hong Kong, and renamed CLAN MACBOYD. *17.9.1984* left Singapore and *1.10.1984* arrived Shanghai breakers.

245. CLAN FINLAY (1962–1968)
O.N. 304143. 9077 g. 4875 n. 461.0x62.3x37.6 ft.
6-cyl. 2SCSA Sulzer oil engine by Wallsend Slipway & Engineering Co. Ltd., Wallsend, 7700bhp.
29.6.1962 launched by Lady Muir and *10.1962* completed by Swan, Hunter & Wigham Richardson Ltd., Wallsend (Yard No.1933) for The Clan Line Steamers Ltd. *1968* sold to Arya National Shipping Line, Iran, and renamed ARYA FAR. *1971* sold to Tat On Shipping, Somali, and renamed ATLANTIC OCEAN. *1975* sold to China Ocean Shipping Co., Guangzhou, China, and renamed LU CHUN.

246. CLAN MACGREGOR (3) (1962–1982)
O.N. 304151. 8811 g. 4909 n. 471.0x63.0x37.7 ft.
6-cyl. 2SCSA Sulzer oil engine by Barclay, Curle & Co. Ltd., Glasgow, 8500bhp.
26.9.1962 launched by Mrs A.H. Gurr and *12.1962* completed by Greenock Dockyard Co. Ltd., Greenock (Yard No.501) for The Clan Line Steamers Ltd. *1969* registered under King Line Ltd. *17.9.1972* in collision with Japanese tanker GENMAR while berthing at Madras, slightly damaged. *1977* registered under The Clan Line Steamers Ltd. *1982* sold to Raft Shipping Co., Greece, and renamed ANGELIKA R. *9.11.1982* on fire 60 miles south of Cyprus, towed to Larnaca, total loss. *3.1983* arrived Laurium, Greece, for scrapping.

247. CLAN MACGOWAN (1963–1970)
O.N. 304153. 8811 g. 4909 n. 471.0x63.0x37.7 ft.
6-cyl. 2SCSA Sulzer oil engine by Wallsend Slipway & Engineering Co. Ltd., Wallsend, 8500bhp.
14.12.1962 launched by Mrs Marples, wife of the Minister of Transport, and *4.1963* completed by Greenock Dockyard Co. Ltd., Greenock (Yard No.502) for The Clan Line Steamers Ltd. *1969* registered under King Line Ltd. *1970* sold to India Steamship Co. Ltd. and renamed INDIAN TRIBUNE. *16.4.1979* severely damaged when struck by Swedish BANDAR ABBAS EXPRESS 9000/78 while berthed at Bombay, repaired. *24.5.1984* laid-up at Calcutta and subsequently scrapped there.

248. CLAN RAMSAY (1965–1980)
O.N. 304194. 7955 g. 4272 n. 485.4x68.6x43.1 ft.
7-cyl. 2SCSA B&W oil engine by J.G. Kincaid & Co. Ltd., Greenock, 10350bhp.
26.8.1964 launched by Countess of Dalhousie and *3.1965* completed by Greenock Dockyard Co. Ltd., Greenock (Yard No.506) for Union-Castle Mail Steamship Co. Ltd. *1977* renamed WINCHESTER CASTLE. *1979* renamed WINCHESTER UNIVERSAL. *1980* sold to Braganza Bay Shipping Co., Greece, and renamed LADY MADONNA. *25.4.1985* arrived Gadani Beach breakers.

249. CLAN RANALD (4) (1965–1981)
O.N. 307627. 7955 g. 4272 n. 485.4x68.6x43.1 ft..
7-cyl. 2SCSA B&W oil engine by J.G. Kincaid & Co. Ltd., Greenock, 10350bhp.
21.12.1964 launched by Mrs A. Paxton and *6.1965* completed by Greenock Dockyard Co. Ltd., Greenock (Yard No.507) for Union-Castle Mail Steamship Co. Ltd. *1977* renamed DOVER CASTLE. *1979* renamed DOVER UNIVERSAL. *1981* sold to Invergordon Shipping Co., Greece, and renamed GOLDEN SEA. *9.5.1985* arrived Gadani Beach from Jeddah for scrapping.

250. CLAN ROBERTSON (4) (1965–1982)
O.N. 307638. 7955 g. 4272 n. 485.4x68.6x43.1 ft.
7-cyl. B&W 2SCSA oil engine by J.G. Kincaid & Co. Ltd., Greenock, 10350bhp.
3.5.1965 launched by Mrs E.R. Duggan and *11.1965* completed by Greenock Dockyard Co. Ltd., Greenock (Yard No.508) for Union-Castle Mail Steamship Co. Ltd. *1977* renamed BALMORAL CASTLE. *1979* renamed BALMORAL UNIVERSAL. *1982* sold to National History Cia Naviera SA, Greece, and renamed PSARA REEFER. *19.6.1984* arrived Chittagong breakers.

251. CLAN ROSS (4) (1966–1982)
O.N. 307645. 7955 g. 4272 n. 485.4x68.6x43.1 ft.
7-cyl. 2SCSA B&W oil engine by J.G. Kincaid & Co. Ltd., Greenock, 10350bhp.
24.9.1965 launched by Mrs R. Hart and *3.1966* completed by Greenock Dockyard Co. Ltd., Greenock (Yard No.509) for Houston Line Ltd. (Cayzer, Irvine & Co. Ltd., managers). *1976* registered under Union-Castle Mail Steamship Co. Ltd. and renamed KINPURNIE CASTLE. *1979* renamed KINPURNIE UNIVERSAL. *1982* sold to National History Cia Naviera SA, Greece, and renamed SYROS REEFER. *31.7.1984* arrived Chittagong breakers.

252. CLAN ALPINE (5) (1967–1981)
O.N. 307670. 8713 g. 4798 n. 470.9x63.0x37.7 ft.
6-cyl. 2SCSA B&W oil engine by J.G. Kincaid & Co. Ltd., Greenock, 8500bhp.
1.12.1966 launched by Miss Elizabeth Cayzer and *4.1967* completed by Scotts Shipbuilding & Engineering Co. Ltd., Greenock (Yard No.708) for The Clan Line Steamers Ltd. *1981* sold to Delibra Shipping Co. Inc., Liberia, and renamed AFRICAN DIAMOND. *1982* renamed PACIFIC AMBER. *2.5.1984* arrived Kaohsiung breakers.

APPENDIX 2
VESSELS MANAGED ON BEHALF OF THE MINISTRY OF WAR TRANSPORT

M1. EMPIRE SONG (1940–1941)
O.N. 166991. 9228 g. 4950 n. 463.8x63.0x29.9 ft.
Two T.3-cyl. with LP exhaust turbines by J.G. Kincaid & Co. Ltd., Greenock, twin screw, 1370nhp.
18.6.1940 launched and *1940* completed by Greenock Dockyard Co. Ltd., Greenock (Yard No.443) as EMPIRE SONG for the Ministry of Shipping. Cayzer, Irvine & Co. Ltd. appointed managers. *9.5.1941* mined and sunk in the Mediterranean near the island of Pantelleria while on a Malta convoy from Gibraltar.

M2. DESIRADE (1940–1945)
O.N. 168811. 9645 g. 6018 n. 483.4x58.9x34.6 ft.
Two T.3-cyl. by shipbuilders, twin screw, 679nhp.
1921 completed by Ateliers & Chanteliers de France, Dunkirk (Yard No.101) as DESIRADE for Cie de Chargeurs Reunis. *1940* taken over by the Ministry of Shipping, later Ministry of War Transport. Cayzer, Irvine & Co. Ltd. appointed managers. *1945* returned to owners. *9.9.1950* left Bordeaux in tow for Bruges to be scrapped by Van Heyghen Freres.

M3. VILLE D'AMIENS (1940–1944)
O.N. 166317. 6975 g. 4216 n. 411.0x53.7x35.8 ft.
T.3-cyl. with LP exhaust turbine by J.G. Kincaid & Co. Ltd., Glasgow, 721nhp.
11.1924 completed by North of Ireland Shipbuilders, Londonderry (Yard No.98) as VILLE D'AMIENS for Cie Havraise Peninsulaire de Navegacione à Vapeurs, Havre. *1940* taken over by Ministry of Shipping, later Ministry of War Transport. Cayzer, Irvine & Co. Ltd. appointed managers. *1944* returned to owners. *1953* scrapped.

M4. LIEUTENANT ST. LOUBERT BIE (1940–1946)
O.N. 168238. 6126 g. 3460 n. 451.0x57.2x27.3 ft.
T.3-cyl. with LP exhaust turbine by shipbuilders, 697nhp.
11.1911 completed by J.C. Tecklenborg, Wesermunde (Yard No.244) as MANNHEIM for Deutsch-Australian Dampfsch, Hamburg. *1919* transferred to the French Government as war reparations. *1922* sold to Messageries Maritime, France, and renamed LIEUTENANT ST. LOUBERT BIE. *1940* taken over by the Ministry of Shipping, later Ministry of War Transport. Cayzer, Irvine & Co. Ltd. appointed managers. *1946* returned to owners. *6.9.1950* arrived La Seyne for scrapping.

M5. ROBERT MAERSK (1940–1944)
O.N. 166210. 2290 g. 1346 n. 327.2x46.2x17.9 ft.
6-cyl. 4SCSA oil engine by Burmeister & Wain, Copenhagen, 355bhp.
2.1937 completed by Odense Staalskibsvft, Odense (Yard No.64) as ROBERT MAERSK for A.P. Moller A/S, Copenhagen. *1940* taken over by Ministry of Shipping, later Ministry of War Transport. Cayzer, Irvine & Co. Ltd. appointed managers. *1944* management transferred to T. & J. Brocklebank, Liverpool. *1946* returned to owners.

1955 sold to Jutlandia D/S A/S, Copenhagen, and renamed BIRGITTE TOFT. *1958* sold to Cathay Shipping Co. Ltd., Singapore, and renamed EVER GLORY. *1967* sold and renamed SINGAPORE PEARL. *1968* sold to State Marine Enterprises SA, Panama, and renamed TANDJUNG LAYANG. *3.4.1970* arrived Hong Kong to be scrapped by Leung Yau Shipbreaking Co.

M6. EMPIRE ELAINE (1942–1947)
O.N. 167744. 7513 g. 5133 n. 416.0x66.7x31.0 ft.
3-cyl. 2SCSA oil engine by W. Doxford & Sons Ltd., Sunderland, 516nhp.
11.1942 completed by Vickers Armstrong Ltd., Barrow (Yard No.856) as EMPIRE ELAINE for the Ministry of War Transport. Cayzer, Irvine & Co. Ltd. appointed managers. *1947* sold to Marine Enterprises Ltd., London, and renamed JOHN LYRAS. *1970* sold to New Frontier Shipping Co., Panama, and renamed BOUNDARY. Arrived Kaohsiung for scrapping prior to *9.9.1972.*

M7. EMPIRE WISDOM (1942–1945)
O.N. 168989. 9205 g. 5065 n. 463.8x63.0x29.9 ft.
Two T.3-cyl. with LP exhaust turbines by J.G. Kincaid & Co. Ltd., Greenock, DR gearing driving twin screws, 1372nhp. *1961* re-engined with two 5-cyl. MAN 2SCSA oil engines by Bremer Vulkan, Vegesack, 9000bhp.
29.7.1942 launched and *11.1942* completed by Greenock Dockyard Co. Ltd., Greenock (Yard No.451) as EMPIRE WISDOM for the Ministry of War Transport. Cayzer, Irvine & Co. Ltd. appointed managers. *1944* management transferred to Blue Star Line Ltd., London. *19.9.1946* sold to Union Cold Storage Co. Ltd. (Blue Star Line, managers) and renamed ROYAL STAR. *1950* owners restyled as Union International Co. Ltd. *1961* transferred to Blue Star Line Ltd., converted to a motor ship and renamed CALEDONIA STAR. *9.12.1971* handed over to Kaohsiung breakers, demolition complete by *25.2.1972.*

M8. ADOLPH S. OCHS (1943–1948)
O.N. 169658. 7219 g. 4380 n. 441.6x56.9x37.4 ft.
T.3-cyl. by General Machinery Corporation, Hamilton, Ohio, 2500ihp.
1943 launched as ADOLPH S. OCHS and *10.1943* completed as SAMWYO by Bethlehem-Fairfield Shipbuilders, Baltimore (Yard No.2239) for the Ministry of War Transport. Cayzer, Irvine & Co. Ltd. appointed managers. *1943* reverted to ADOLPH S. OCHS. *1948* returned to the USA. *12.1968* scrapped at Kearney, New Jersey.

M9. SAMAYE (1943–1947)
O.N. 180496. 7219 g. 4380 n. 441.6x56.9x37.4 ft.
T.3-cyl. by Worthington Pump & Machinery Corporation, Harrison, New Jersey, 2500ihp.
1943 launched as JAMES T. EARLE and *9.1943* completed as SAMAYE by Bethlehem-Fairfield Shipbuilders, Baltimore (Yard No.2223) for the Ministry of War Transport. Cayzer, Irvine & Co. Ltd. appointed managers, *1947* sold to T. Dunlop, London, and renamed QUEEN VICTORIA. *1948* sold to T. & J. Harrison, Liverpool, and renamed HISTORIAN. *12.1962* sold to Jayanti Shipping Co., India, and renamed PARVATI JAYANTI. *6.9.1967* damaged by Israeli gunfire in Suez Harbour during Arab–Israeli war, repaired. *22.2.1968* aground at Azemmour, 50 miles from Casablanca, while on a voyage from Alexandria to Bombay with cotton. *23.2.1968* refloated, seriously damaged. *4.1968* scrapped at Aviles.

M10. SAMBALT (1943–1947)
O.N. 169766. 7219 g. 4380 n. 441.6x56.9x37.4 ft.
T.3-cyl. by General Machinery Corporation, Hamilton, Ohio, 2500ihp.
1943 launched as ROBERT WICKLIFFE and *12.1943* completed as SAMBALT by Bethlehem-Fairfield Shipbuilders, Baltimore (Yard No.2290) for the Ministry of War Transport. Cayzer, Irvine & Co. Ltd. appointed managers. *1947* sold to Mollers Ltd., Hong Kong, and renamed LILIAN MOLLER. *1948* sold to T. & J. Harrison, Liverpool, and renamed SPEAKER. *3.1962* sold to Epos Marine Enterprises SA, Panama, and renamed BYZANTION. *5.1969* scrapped Onomichi, Japan.

M11. SAMBRIAN (1943–1947). See CLAN MACFARLANE (3) No.195.

M12. SAMCHESS (1944–1947)
O.N. 169823. 7219 g. 4380 n. 441.6x56.9x37.4 ft.
T.3-cyl. by General Machinery Corporation, Hamilton, Ohio, 2500ihp.
1.1944 completed as SAMCHESS by Bethlehem-Fairfield Shipbuilders, Baltimore (Yard No.2312) for the Ministry of War Transport. Cayzer, Irvine & Co. Ltd. appointed managers. *1947* sold to Alpha South African Steamship Co. Ltd., London, and renamed ALPHA MOOI. *1948* sold to Somerset Steamship Co. Ltd., London (Counties Ship Management Ltd.) and renamed PORLOCK HILL. *21.12.1951* ashore two miles SE of Famagusta in a gale, on a voyage from Southampton to Port Said with army stores. *22.12.1951* broke in two, total loss. *29.4.1952* towed to Alexandria and unloaded. *14.5.1952* towed to Palermo and scrapped.

M13. SAMDERWENT (1944–1947). See CLAN MACFAYDEN (3) No.194.

M14. SAMDON (1943–1946)
O.N. 169781. 7219 g. 4380 n. 441.6x56.9x37.4 ft.
T.3-cyl. by Harrisburg Machinery Corporation, Harrisburg, Pennsylvania, 2500ihp.
12.1943 completed by New England Shipbuilding Corporation, Portland, Maine (Yard No.2210) as SAMDON for the Ministry of War Transport. Cayzer, Irvine & Co. Ltd. appointed managers. *1946* returned to the USA. *10.1961* scrapped at Philadelphia.

M15. SAMFIELD (1943–1947)
O.N. 169765. 7219 g. 4380 n. 441.6x56.9x37.4 ft.
T.3-cyl. by Worthington Pump & Machinery Co., Harrison, New Jersey, 2500ihp.
1943 launched as DANIEL APPLETON and *11.1943* completed as SAMFIELD by Bethlehem-Fairfield Shipbuilders, Baltimore (Yard No.2276) for the Ministry of War Transport. Cayzer, Irvine & Co. Ltd. appointed managers. *1947* sold to Moor Line Ltd., London (W. Runciman & Co. Ltd., managers) and renamed SOUTHMOOR. *1950* sold and renamed MARINE PRIDE. *1951* sold to Mar del Sur Compania Naviera SA, Costa Rica, and renamed ST. SPERO. *1953* sold to Luciferus Cia Maritima SA, Costa Rica, and renamed ENDEAVOUR. *1959* sold to Ocean Span Corporation, Monrovia, and renamed VALIANT LIBERTY. *1960* sold and renamed SKYLLAS. *1960* sold to Taiwan Ming Sung Industrial Co. Ltd., Keelung, and renamed HWEI SUNG. *30.10.1961* aground at Naoyetsu, Honshu, while discharging. *7.11.1961* refloated, constructive total loss. *2.1962* scrapped Osaka.

M16. SAMNEBRA (1943–1947)
O.N. 169655. 7219 g. 4380 n. 441.6x56.9x37.4 ft.
T.3-cyl. by General Machinery Corporation, Hamilton, Ohio, 2500ihp.
1943 launched as LYON G. TYLER and *10.1943* completed as SAMNEBRA by Bethlehem-Fairfield Shipbuilders, Baltimore (Yard No.2247) for the Ministry of War Transport. Cayzer, Irvine & Co. Ltd. appointed managers. *1947* sold to Chellew Navigation Co. Ltd., London, and renamed PENTIRE. *1955* sold to Cie de Nav. Gaviota SA, Panama, and renamed CUACO. *6.1963* scrapped Hirao.

M17. SAMOKLA (1943–1948)
O.N. 169698. 7219 g. 4380 n. 441.6x56.9x37.4 ft.
T.3-cyl. by General Machinery Corporation, Hamilton, Ohio, 2500ihp.
1943 launched as JOSE ARTIGAS and *11.1943* completed as SAMOKLA by Bethlehem-Fairfield Shipbuilders, Baltimore (Yard No.2260) for the Ministry of War Transport. Cayzer, Irvine & Co. Ltd. appointed managers. *1948* returned to the USA. *1962* scrapped at Newport News, Virginia.

M18. SAMPENN (1943–1948)
O.N. 169633. 7219 g. 4380 n. 441.6x56.9x37.4 ft.
T.3-cyl. by General Machinery Corporation, Hamilton, Ohio, 2500ihp.
1943 launched as JOHN H. HATTON and *9.1943* completed as SAMORA by Bethlehem-Fairfield Shipbuilders, Baltimore (Yard No.2224) for the Ministry of War Transport. Cayzer, Irvine & Co. Ltd. appointed managers. *1943* renamed SAMPENN. *1948* returned to the USA. *9.1966* scrapped at New Orleans.

M19. SAMPORT (1943–1948)
O.N. 169786. 7219 g. 4380 n. 441.6x56.9x37.4 ft.
T.3-cyl. by General Machinery Corporation, Hamilton, Ohio, 2500ihp.
1943 launched as ISRAEL WHEELEN and *12.1943* completed as SAMPORT by Bethlehem-Fairfield Shipbuilders, Baltimore (Yard No.2287) for the Ministry of War Transport. Cayzer, Irvine & Co. Ltd. appointed managers. *1948* returned to the USA as ISRAEL WHEELEN. *11.1962* scrapped at Panama City, Florida.

M20. BANGKOK II (1943–1946)
O.N. 168828. 8056 g. 5077 n. 445.0x58.0x37.3 ft.
Two T.3-cyl. by shipbuilder, 516nhp, twin screws.
12.1919 completed by Uraga Dock Co. Ltd., Uraga (Yard No.144) as BANGKOK for Societe Navigacione à Vapeurs France – Indo-Chine. *1934* sold to Chargeurs Reunis, Dunkirk, name unchanged. *1942* renamed BANGKOK II. *1943* taken over by the Ministry of War Transport. Cayzer, Irvine & Co. Ltd. appointed managers. *1946* returned to owners, renamed BANGKOK. *1954* scrapped.

M21. COMMANDANT DORISE (1943–1946)
O.N. 167854. 5529 g. 3470 n. 400.4x54.5x27.4 ft.
T.3-cyl. by shipbuilder, 510nhp.
6.1917 completed by Mitsubishi Dockyard and Engine Works, Kobe (Yard No.66) for Messageries Maritime, France, as COMMANDANT DORISE. *1943* taken over by the Ministry of War Transport. Cayzer, Irvine & Co. Ltd. appointed managers. *1946* returned to owners. *1951* sold to Pierre Atychides, Piraeus, renamed MARO.

1954 sold to Kenfig Steamship Co. Ltd., London (S. Catsell & Co., managers), renamed SAN NICOLAS. *1955* sold to Cia de Nav. San Antonio Ltda, Costa Rica, renamed SAN NICOLAS II. *23.3.1959* arrived Hong Kong for scrapping by Mollers Ltd. Last trip made under the British flag.

M22. EMPIRE MALTA (1944–1946)
O.N. 180072. 3610 g. 2265 n. 315.5x46.5x22.1 ft.
T.3-cyl. by Central Marine Engine Works, West Hartlepool, 299nhp.
5.1944 completed by W. Gray & Co. Ltd., West Hartlepool (Yard No.1167) as EMPIRE MALTA for the Ministry of War Transport. Cayzer, Irvine & Co. Ltd. appointed managers. *1946* sold to Indo-China Steam Navigation Co. Ltd., Hong Kong, and renamed HANGSANG. *1960* sold to Continental Enterprises and Navigation, Hong Kong, and renamed SLIGHT WIND. *1965* sold to Sunbeam Nav. Co. SA, Panama, renamed SUNBEAM. *23.7.1969* engines broken down in position 13° 56'N 114° 30'E while on a voyage from Malaysia to Kaohsiung, towed to her destination and laid-up. *1970* scrapped Kaohsiung.

M23. EMPIRE PERLIS (1944–1946)
O.N. 180074. 3610 g. 2265 n. 315.5x46.5x22.1 ft.
T.3-cyl. by Central Marine Engine Works, West Hartlepool, 299nhp.
7.1944 completed by W. Gray & Co. Ltd., West Hartlepool (Yard No.1168) as EMPIRE PERLIS for the Ministry of War Transport. Cayzer, Irvine & Co. Ltd. appointed managers. *1946* sold to Indo-China Steam Navigation Co. Ltd., Hong Kong, and renamed HINSANG. *1965* sold to Kinabatangan Shipping Co. Ltd., Hong Kong, and renamed KOWLOON. *1969* sold to Concordia Kinabatangan Shipping SA, Panama, and renamed HORIS. *29.12.1969* foundered in position 3° 53'N 119° 23'E while on a voyage from Surabaja to Hong Kong in heavy weather after developing leaks shortly after leaving Surabaja.

M24. EMPIRE PRINCE (1944–1945). See CLAN ANGUS No.182.

M25. EMPIRE BARRIE (1944–1945). See CLAN ALPINE (4) No.183.

M26. EMPIRE FOREST (1944–1946). See CLAN ALLAN No.187.

M27. EMPIRE FAWLEY (1945–1946). See CLAN MACKINLAY (2) No.184.

M28. EMPIRE DUNNET (1945–1946) .See CLAN MACKINNON (3) No.185.

M29. EMPIRE GUNFLEET (1945–1946). See CLAN MACKAY (5) No.186.

M30. HOOGKERK (1945–1947)
O.N. 143311. 5125 g. 3205 n. 410.0x54.7x26.7 ft.
Q.4-cyl. by shipbuilders, 563nhp.

9.1911 completed by Flensburger Schiffs, Flensburg (Yard No.312) as ATTO for Roland Linie Akt. Bremen. *1921* sold to David Steamship Co. Ltd., London, and renamed ST. AUGUSTINE ABBEY. *1922* sold to Vereenigde Nederlandsche Scheeps Maats and renamed HOOGKERK. *1945* taken over by the Ministry of War Transport. Cayzer, Irvine & Co. Ltd. appointed managers. *1947* returned to owners. *1949* sold to Royal Netherlands Government and renamed VETERAAN. *4.1958* scrapped by Simons & Co., Rotterdam.

M31. OCEAN GLORY (1946–1948). See CLAN MACBETH (2) No.206.

M32. EMPIRE CATO (1946–1948). See CLAN MACKENZIE (4) No.207.

M33. EMPIRE PICKWICK (1946–1948). See CLAN MACKENDRICK No.208.

M34. EMPIRE LANKESTER (1946–1948). See CLAN MACKELLAR (2) No.209.

M35. EMPIRE CANUTE (1947)
O.N. 212245. 7750 g. 4475 n. 451.0x66.7x31.0 ft.
Steam Turbine connected to electric motor by General Electric Co., Erith. *1954* re-engined with 8-cyl. 2SCSA oil engine by Bremer-Vulkan, Vegesack.
6.1947 completed by Greenock Dockyard Co. Ltd., Greenock (Yard No.462) as EMPIRE CANUTE for the Ministry of War Transport. Cayzer, Irvine & Co. Ltd. appointed managers. *1947* sold to Belships Co. Ltd. Skibs A/S (Christen Smith, manager), Norway, and renamed BELOCEAN. *1964* sold to Bacong Shipping Co., Panama, and renamed SOUTHERN STAR. *1967* sold to Manila Interocean Lines Inc., Philippines, and renamed MARIE ANN. *28.7.1976* left Karachi for Gadani Beach for scrapping.

CLAN LINE FLEET INDEX